Voicemails from My Sister:
Stories of A Schizoaffective Sibling

An account of my relationship with my sister. The good, the bad, the hilarious.

by
Kate Russell

Amazon.com

Copyright © 2021 Kate Russell

All rights reserved.

Table of Contents

1) What's Wrong?
2) Baby
3) Opposites
4) Psych Wards
5) Sister Mom
6) Lilith Fair
7) Alternative Education
8) Dad Tries
9) I Try
10) Ward of the State
11) Sibby's Resume
12) The End of Make Believe
13) Michael
14) Duck Muffin
15) Fishing
16) Basket Tossing
17) Alateen
18) You Can't Trust Your Friends
19) Got God?
20) Never Mix, Never Worry
21) Vampire
22) Six Flags
23) The Halloween Party
24) Creative Solutions
25) All Better?
26) Gina & Tanesha
27) Progress
28) Sibby's "Moving"
29) Investing in Friendship
30) Tom
31) Hoarding
32) Squatters
33) You Can't Have Nice Things

34) Scattered
35) Conspiracy Theories
36) Sibby the Celebrity
37) Sibby's LA Visit
38) Shifty, Where Are You?
39) Raging Waters
40) Spiritual Solution
41) Sibby Makes The Blotter
42) Derek
43) My Package
44) Striphilus
45) Ghost Baby
46) Blocking The Crazy
47) Rape Baby
48) Do You Want the Good News or the Bad News?
49) I'm Sorry
50) It's Only Getting Worse
51) I Get It
52) What it's Like Now

Voicemails from My Sister

Chapter 1
What's Wrong?

"Sibby's weird. What's wrong with her?" That's what people asked about my five-year old sister.

Well, I'll tell you. She was dealt an unfair hand.

Our mother, Denise, was an addict. Cocaine, vodka, and cigarettes made up my sister's in utero diet. You see, she'd tested the theory that drugs and alcohol don't hurt fetuses on me. *I* had come out "fine," so she surmised doctors were all a bunch of hippy dippy liberals spouting a bunch of new age hooey, and indulged heavily during her second pregnancy. When Siobhan popped out "cute," and "not retarded," as my father lovingly put it, my parents concluded, brilliantly, that she was normal, and absolved themselves of any and all responsibility from thereon out.

But she was *not* normal. Sibby was cognitively impaired as a result of my parents decision to abuse her in the womb. She was developmentally disabled, and had intellectual disabilities. In other words, her brain wasn't developing normally.

Our father, Ed, a narcissistic workaholic, worked nights as a stagehand while our mother, an alcoholic, drank and resentfully brainwashed her new favorite infant. I'd hear her slurring to my baby sister, "Buddha is your real father. Eddie is Kate's daddy, but *they're* nothing. *You* are special. *You're* my angel baby." My young sister soaked up the belligerence like a sponge, believing every word, and her skewed perspective of the world began to form.

Voicemails from My Sister

As soon as Sibby started preschool, her teachers noticed something was wrong. She was having a hard time paying attention, and had unusual social skills. They determined she had Attention Deficit Hyperactivity Disorder. It was the 80's. ADHD was the diagnosis of the times. They put her on Ritalin.

Sibby continued to develop abnormally, and our parents committed to the belief that she was simply acting out. She could barely sit still in school, and never did her work. My mother, too drunk to help her with homework, instead showered her with praise while in her nightly blackouts. "You are so beautiful, you could be a model." She sculpted Sibby's brain to believe that her looks would lead her to prosperity, and her intelligence and skill set were irrelevant.

Meanwhile, Sibby struggled to make friends, and failed academically at school. Extended family, unable or unwilling to help, passive-aggressively inquired about her status.

Attempting to make light of a heavy situation, our cousin nicknamed Sibby a cute-sounding insult. "How's Sibnuts?" she asked as we lay by the pool one day.

I exhaled a heavy sigh. "Crazy," I responded.

Chapter 2
Baby

Siobhan was the cutest baby in the whole wide world. She had dimples and brown ringlets. Her head was completely round and she had big brown eyes. She was perfectly chubby with squishy pink cheeks. I was five when she was born, and immediately I was in love. I couldn't look at her without wanting to pick her up and smother her with kisses.

She had a giggle that would melt your heart. Our parents bought her a wind-up swing; my mother and I would sit in front of it and, every third or fourth time it'd swing towards us, I'd exclaim, "Buggala buggala boo," and tickle her. She'd explode in chuckles every time. Our mother bought a handheld tape recorder with mini cassette tapes just to record that laugh for my dad when he got home from work.

I used to lay her on her stomach on this plastic hippopotamus on wheels, and roll her down the hallway. I stayed over her, like a parent guiding their child on a bike for the first time without training wheels. She'd try to hold her arms and legs up, so it looked like she was flying, which made her tongue stick out of her mouth as if she were concentrating. She looked like a crazy old man, complete with wrinkled forehead.

My favorite picture of us is me feeding her a bottle when she was just an infant and I was five. I'm cradling her in my arms, staring lovingly at her innocent little face.

She had the cutest little round butt, and I'd spontaneously yell, "Booty!" and chase her around the house singing, "I'm gonna squish it, I'm gonna squash it, I'm gonna jooce it!"

Voicemails from My Sister

Once I'd pinched her butt, she became "it," and would turn around to chase *me* and squeeze *my* butt.

No matter how bad a day I was having, hugging Siobhan fixed it. Holding that baby always made me smile. She filled my heart.

At night I'd sing her a lullaby that our nana used to sing to me:

"Baby's boat's a silver moon
Sailing in the sky,
Sailing o're a sea of sleep
As the clouds roll by.
Sail baby sail,
Out upon the sea
Only don't forget to sail
Back again to me."

Chapter 3
Opposites

Although cut from the same cloth, Sibby and I were completely different. I was a good girl, she was a hell-raiser.

Our abusive parents frightened me into behaving. Sibby, on the other hand, could not be scared into submission.

"Punkie," our father would holler to me. (Not sure where my childhood nickname came from, but it pre-dated Punky Brewster.) "Make your bed!" I'd immediately obey. "Sibby, put your toys away," he'd command my sister. Giving him a querulous look, she'd turn and stomp away to sulk in a corner.

I was neat, Sibby was messy. I was fastidious, Sibby was careless.

When I was eight and Sibby three, our parents dressed us up as an angel and a devil for Halloween. Seraphic and sanguine by nature, I wore my white sheet and wings with a smile. Petulant and irritable, Sibby tugged at her horns until they fell off.

Whereas I hung around with the well-behaved kids, Sibby befriended the delinquents.

While I did well in school, Sibby was held back so many times she was forced to attend an alternative school.

I was blond, short, and chubby. Sibby tall, brunette, and thin.

We were opposites in every way you could imagine.

Chapter 4
Psych Wards

Siobhan visited her first psych ward when she was nine years old. In 1993, after much debate with our father, who stood firm in his belief that mental illness was "not a thing," our mother convinced him to swallow the out-of-pocket co-pay for fourteen days in Yale New Haven Hospital's Institute of Living. This stint began Sibby's lifelong relationship with mental illness facilities.

She was assigned to a two-person room with a suicidally depressed eight-year-old girl. Next door was a small padded cell where the girls were encouraged to go when their rage became socially unacceptable, so that they could take their anger out on the environment instead of each other. Sibby spent at least an hour a day in that room, beating the walls and crying.

Since Ed and Denise avoided mentioning to Sibby's doctors that she had been subjected to drugs and alcohol in the womb, the fourteen-day hospitalization resulted in the conclusion that the only thing wrong with Siobhan was that she had Lyme disease. Mood swings and an inability to concentrate were symptoms of Lyme Disease. Phew. That diagnosis fit the narrative *and* allowed my parents to remain guilt-free. They fed her some Amoxicillin and painted themselves as A+ parents.

The Institute of Living had a jail-like vibe, at least as far as Sibby was concerned. Strict, regimented, and no-nonsense, this facility was a far cry from her undisciplined home life, where she was left to her own devices. Her stay surrounded Christmas, but they let her out on a one-day furlough so she could pretend to be happy with her strained family. As is common with children of alcoholics, Sibby was a people-pleaser, smiling through her pain when in the presence of our abusive parents. Pretending to be happy when she knew she was supposed to be, for their sakes.

A couple years after her in-patient stay at IOL, Sibby was recommended to the Coping Center at Connecticut Children's hospital for talk therapy. Her still-improperly-diagnosed "condition" seemed to be getting worse, not better. She couldn't focus, despite the prescriptions she was taking, and she'd become weirdly aggressive, hissing at her classmates like a cat. After a few brief group counseling sessions, our parents refused to drive her to this facility anymore. After all, Hartford was thirty minutes away, and the sessions hadn't fixed her yet, so they must not be working. Our parents expected treatment to work like drugs — instantly. When therapy proved to be a lifelong process, they wrote it off as bullshit.

In 1997, Sibby and our dad had a fight and the police were called. No one was arrested, but the matter went to family court. The judge mandated Dad and Siobhan to a whopping three sessions of family counseling. As if that'd do the trick. Spoiler alert — it didn't.

Siobhan continued her sporadic intervals of psychotherapy at the community health center, for which our father begrudgingly paid the sliding scale fees. As far as he was concerned, Siobhan's problems were all behavioral, and she could get in line if she so chose. Cognitive impairment wasn't a thing, and he certainly wasn't responsible for any of Sibby's problems, how dare you even suggest it!

At fifteen, she began attending Rushford's Respite Care Program. Respite is "temporary care provided to a child for the short-term relief of a caregiver." In this case, our parents. That's right. Ed and Denise honestly believed that they had done *so* much for Sibby that they deserved a state-funded break. She attended this program three times a week after school, where she befriended other neglected children of addicts.

Not surprisingly, she wound up back in The Institute of Living in 2000 for another two-week stay. It was obvious to everyone except our in-denial parents that something was medically wrong with Sibby. Her brain simply wasn't developing correctly. Of course it wasn't. You can't feed a growing fetus cocaine and alcohol and expect it to develop healthily.

My dad and I visited Sibby at IOL the day before her sweet sixteen. He was in one of his despondent, it's-all-about-me moods, sulking in silence most of the time. As is normal for Al-anons, children of addicts who have been programed to try to make their parents happy, Sibby and I directed all of our energy toward trying to pull him out of his poopy mood. She suggested the three of us play Talk it Out, a self-help board game that encourages communication.

My father drew a card that read, *What do you like to do with your friends?*

"I don't have any fucking friends," he muttered, slamming the card down.

Sibby and I laughed nervously, because that's the way we'd been taught to respond to situations that made us uncomfortable. Suddenly no one wanted to play anymore. Our narcissistic father couldn't stop navel-gazing for five minutes for the sake of his children.

Voicemails from My Sister

At seventeen Sibby began seeking outpatient treatment at Elmcrest, a children's psychiatric facility in Portland, CT. She was frantic, riddled with anxiety, and prone to panic attacks at this point. Her temper was so short that I couldn't even spend five minutes with her without her exploding on me. "Watch the road!" she'd often exclaim from the passenger seat. I *had* been. She was just terrified of everything.

A few months later, she took a "hair test" that my herbalist recommended. I'd gone to this hippie medicine man for my acne, but he ended up becoming a sort of therapist to me, and I talked to him about my troubled sister.

"I suspect she has mercury poisoning. That can cause numerous health problems."

She snipped a small patch of her pubic hair and mailed it into a testing facility. When we got the results, she was off the charts with heavy metal poisoning, likely from years of various psychiatric medications. Unfortunately, she was unable to follow through with his recommended treatment plan of an organic diet and vitamins. My father scoffed at the notion of driving her into the woods of Hebron once a month to visit this gypsy, then shelling out his hard-earned money for loose-leaf tea. Plus, as a vampire, Sibby refused to eat garlic (more on this later).

In 2006, at twenty-one years old, Sibby was sentenced to Connecticut Valley Hospital after biting our mother. CVH is the involuntary state psychiatric hospital, ironically located directly across the street from our house. Seriously. She was there for a month. The doctors rearranged her cocktail of psych meds and changed the dosages.

Voicemails from My Sister

I had been living in California, three-thousand miles away from the chaos, for two years at this point. While locked up in the mental ward, she wrote me a letter.

> *I pissed off the police so bad in this town that I'm being banished. I'm feeling better. If I don't speak about "it" I'll be fine* (I don't know what "it" was)*. I got drunk and said some things I shouldn't of. There. Thats [sic] as much as I can tell you. I'm looking into jobs but I only have a one-hour pass in the morning and in the evening. I am repeating myself for good reason. I'm sure if you understand the "M"* (again, no idea what she's talking about) *might actually be protecting me because I gave up the location I shouldn't of.*

A few weeks later, I got another letter. After three weeks of taking her medication regularly (she missed pills all the time when on her own) Sibby was showing some signs of improvement, and they were preparing to release her. Where to, was the question. Our parents had had it with her and would no longer allow her to live with them. A group home seemed the best option. She was clearly incapable of taking care of herself. But alas:

> *Dear Kate, I have something I want you to know. I realize that when we talked we agreed on me going to a group home but I think I'm going to consider my options. In truth I signed into this program when I was 18 and I can't really leave the program. After I receive my benefits I'm going to try to get an apartment. They are pushing me kinda to save money but I might get one with some friend. Not too sure. But I love you very much. Write back soon.*

Voicemails from My Sister

She moved into an apartment by herself. When she could get a ride she attended her weekly therapy sessions at River Valley Services. Oftentimes, however, she had no one to drive her, so she missed these appointments. She also forgot to take her medicine most of the time.

In 2019, Sibby wound up back in CVH after a routine evaluation revealed that she was pregnant. The state had a legal responsibility to ensure Sibby gave birth to a healthy fetus. (If only our mother had received such thorough care.) Over the next six months, Siobhan turned into the healthiest version of herself I'd ever known.

On April 1, 2020, she gave birth to a beautiful, healthy baby boy.

Chapter 5
Sister Mom

I was five years old when Sibby was born, but I immediately became her mother. Our actual mother spent the daytime locked in her bedroom napping off the previous night's party. Our father was at work. So it was my responsibility to wake up with Sibby, change her diaper, give her her bottle and baby food, and play with her quietly until our mother emerged from her room.

Sometimes Sibby would cry, though, as babies do, and I would hold my hand over her mouth, pressing harder and harder while begging her to stop. I had adopted this tactic after our mother threatened to kill us both with a steak knife because Sibby's sobs had woken her up. Fearing for our lives, I employed the only strategy I knew with which to achieve desired results — force. Our parents used it on us, and it had worked on me. Why, then, wouldn't it work on my sister?

Because not all brains are created equal, that's why. Sibby never did respond to violence by snapping into line. She rebelled.

"Sibby, put away your laundry so we can go out," I instructed my eight-year old sister one Saturday afternoon.

"No," she replied.

"Sibby," I warned. "Mom said you have to put away your clothes, so just do it so we can leave."

"No," she repeated.

That was it. I grabbed her, dug my nails into her arms and screamed in her face. "JUST FUCKING DO IT, YOU LITTLE SHIT!"

Her eyes welled up with tears and she whimpered, "No."

I responded to each refusal with more physical force, until I finally stormed out of the room in a rage, leaving her sobbing in a heap on the floor.

Why wouldn't she just do as she was told? As I would go on to learn over the years, her brain just didn't work the same way as mine.

The abuse fizzled out as she got bigger and began fighting back. Still, I mothered to the best of my ability.

I took her to open her first bank account, and to the OBGYN when she became sexually active. I drove her to her doctor's appointments, and bought her school supplies. I showed her how to clean her room, and gave her an allowance out of my own pocket.

But all of this would backfire, as her mental illness would come to turn it into evil deeds instead of good deeds.

Chapter 6
Lilith Fair

In 1997, when Sibby was thirteen and I was eighteen, I invited her to attend the Lilith Fair with me and my two friends.

Sarah McLachlan, Fiona Apple, and Tracy Chapman were slated to perform, and I bought our tickets with my own hard-earned waitressing money.

My sister and I had a somewhat strained relationship at this point, so my invitation was (another) attempt to build a bond between us. We hadn't been close for years. I had been her mother when she was a baby, but when I escaped to my grandmother's house at the age of twelve my mother resumed brainwashing Sibby with lies about how I was a no-good slut who wasn't even her real sister anyway.

Nonetheless, Sibby and I constantly attempted to form a healthy relationship throughout the years. This concert, I was sure, would be a memory we'd hold dear for a lifetime.

Siobhan and I drove to my friend Jocelyn's house in West Hartford full of excited energy. I drove extra carefully that day, as our mother had purchased a six-pack of wine coolers for us, her underage daughters, which I intended to smuggle into the Meadows Music venue in my cheerleading bag. Already a pro at driving under the influence of pot, I knew to hide the bag in the trunk until we arrived. Attempting anything that might strengthen our bond, I shared a few hits of a joint with my young sister as I drove the speed limit to Jocelyn's house. This may sound hypocritical after shaming my mother for her using, but at eighteen I didn't know any better.

Voicemails from My Sister

Jocelyn and Ariel were ready to go when Siobhan and I pulled up, so we transferred into Jocelyn's car and set out on our way. Tori Amos blasted from the CD player and we sung along, lamenting how bummed we were that she wasn't in the lineup. We pulled onto I-84 East. Traffic was heavy. Everyone was headed to the concert.

The stereo was loud. The four of us sang along. Jocelyn, caught up in the excitement, switched lanes to the beat of the music without looking over her shoulder. A flatbed truck was merging into the same lane. I saw it. She did not.

"JOCELYN!"

She panicked as she saw the 18-wheeler merging into our lane. Wrenching the wheel all the way to the left, then all the way to the right, like an inexperienced video gamer playing A2 Racer, she crashed headfirst into the side of the flatbed. My head hit the window.

I heard Sibby scream, "KATE!" Then I blacked out.

The next thing I knew I was being dragged out of the car by two Good Samaritans who'd jumped out of their own car to help. Jocelyn, Ariel, and Siobhan stood crying on the grass a ways away from the highway. They ran to me as the mother and son who pulled me from the totaled car placed me gently on the grass.

"Punkie!" Sibby cried, as she knelt down next to me. "I thought you were dead!"

Through my confusion, I smiled to reassure her. Thank God she was unhurt.

Then I passed out again.

I woke up in the hospital a few hours later, extremely dizzy, with a splitting headache.

Sibby sat between our parents, their arms around her. It was a beautiful picture, despite the circumstances.

"Punkie!" Sibby ran to me. She hugged me too tight.

"Ow!" I cried. My neck felt broken.

"Oh, sorry, sorry. I'm just so glad you're alive!" She broke into loud sobs.

"I'm fine, Sibby." I instinctively tried to calm her down.

I wasn't fine, but her manic overreaction annoyed me.

I was released and spent the next three days in bed recovering. I had been living with Gumma, our paternal grandmother, for six years at that point, and Sibby rarely came over to visit. Gumma loved me more than Sibby, and she could feel it. During this period, however, Sibby came over multiple times a day to check on me.

"I brought you chicken soup," she announced the next morning, holding out a can of Campbells.

"Thank you, Sibs," I replied. She was full of love. And she tried so hard.

Chapter 7
Alternative Education

By the time she reached high school, Sibby had to be placed in an "alternative" school, as she was in danger of being held back *another* year. She had flunked ninth grade once, so halfway through her second go-round her guidance counselor contacted our parents and suggested that Sibby enroll in the Rushford School, to prevent her from becoming a third-year freshman.

This school was designed for kids whose social, emotional, and behavioral needs were not being met by a traditional school. The goal of this dropout diversion program was to teach troubled and learning-disabled kids life skills so they could at least take care of themselves.
 But it should've been called "How to Be a Professional Bum," as Sibby's class was comprised of nine delinquent teenagers walking around Middletown all day looking for bottles and cans to recycle, while smoking cigarettes.

"The teacher lets you smoke?" I exclaimed after Sibby revealed her first semester routine.

"Yeah, she doesn't care."

 I couldn't believe it.

"We made brownies today," she revealed.

"From scratch?" I wondered aloud.

"No, from Duncan Hines."

Voicemails from My Sister

Hey, it was better than nothing.

The program was supposed to focus on each child's individual strengths. Their success was determined by how well they utilized their assets in accomplishing tasks. Completion of the tasks was not a factor in grading. Using their strengths and applying effort were all that was required for success.

It's a nice idea, but unfortunately for Sibby she was so far behind developmentally that she had very few life skills to draw upon. Adding a cup of water to a box of brownie mix and putting it in the oven *was* a huge accomplishment for her. But, be forewarned, — she would forget about them, set off the smoke alarm, and leave a burnt tray of chocolate ash in the oven forever.

I started to see this program for what it really was: a nine-to-two babysitter. Most of the students had arrest records, so this institution kept them out of the way of law enforcement Monday through Friday.

Sibby graduated in 2002. Our mother showed up late to the ceremony, swigging from a large bottle of tonic water.

"You know that's two-thirds vodka," my father whispered to me.

Yeah, I knew.

Chapter 8
Dad Tries

Occasionally Ed tried to be a good father to Sibby. But ultimately his impatience always won out.

Nonetheless, he attempted to bond with his youngest daughter over the years, doing his best to repair the damage that, deep down, he knew he was somewhat responsible for. He'd never admit it out loud, but he was deeply affected by the feeling of having failed as a father.

He'd fall into deep depressions.

"I don't want anything," he mumbled to me on his birthday, a few weeks after Sibby was discharged from her second stint in The Institute of Living in 2000.

So, a few days later, I returned the gifts I'd worked so hard to buy.

It was almost as if his subconscious was nudging him to prove he was capable of compassion when he took in a friend of Sibby's in 2000 and allowed her to live with them for three months.

Ginny Stockwell had been living with her alcoholic mother since her father walked out on them a few months prior. Her mother was abusive and neglectful. Sound familiar? Perhaps because Ed could relate, he took pity on the girl and offered her my old room for as long as she needed. As if to demonstrate how loving he was and convince Siobhan to straighten out and behave once and for all.

Voicemails from My Sister

The arrangement worked out well for a while. Ginny, although from a troubled home, was a positive influence on Siobhan. She didn't have any notable mental disorders, so she was a good example of sanity and balance, which Sibby greatly lacked. Ed was usually at work, so Ginny acted as a sort of built-in babysitter. She was a polite houseguest, who even went the extra mile of cleaning up after my sister. Things were looking up.

I came home from college for Christmas that year. Since Ginny was living with them at that point, our father included her in our family Christmas. Sibby and I watched Ed hand Ginny present after present that he had bought especially for her. It was truly one of the most selfless and beautiful things I've ever witnessed.

Ginny was floored by this generosity, and Sibby and I fought back tears. He had bought her a new book bag, as hers was tattered and worn. He'd purchased her new jeans and tops, outfitting her with an almost entirely new wardrobe. He stuffed a stocking with Ring Pops and Now and Laters, her favorite candies, and gave her a card with $100 bill in it.

"Wow," she exhaled. "I've never gotten so much for Christmas before. Thank you so much."

Siobhan hugged my father and let her tears fall.

But as all good things must come to an end, Ginny and Siobhan began fighting shortly thereafter. Siobhan's mental disorders caused her to resent the instructional tone Ginny took with her.

"You're not my mother!" Sibby would shout at her now ex-best friend. "You don't even live here! Go back to your own house!"

Voicemails from My Sister

After a few days of this, Ginny decided living with her abusive mother was a better option than the current situation, and she returned home, thanking our father for all that he'd done.

Sibby, as would become her habit, pushed away another person who'd tried to help her.

Chapter 9
I Try

When she turned eighteen, my father gave Siobhan two choices: "You can get a job and pay rent, or you can go to community college and live here for free." Six months later, having done neither, he kicked her out.

"My dad said he saw your sister begging for money outside the library," my cousin Elizabeth revealed to me soon after our father 86-ed her. My heart broke.

I resolved to help her. Siobhan was sleeping on a hoodlum friend's couch, but this arrangement was nearing its expiration date. As usually happened with Sibby's relationships, it turned volatile after a few weeks. Or sometimes a few hours.

"Do you want me to help you find an apartment and a job?" I asked my desperate sister in 2003. She was incapable of accomplishing this on her own. We both knew that.

"Yes, thank you, Punkie," she replied, gratefully.

For the next month, every day after work and on my days off, I'd pick Siobhan up at her friend's house and take her apartment and job hunting. I worked on Main Street in Middletown, which was full of options for Sibby. There were tons of businesses and plenty of affordable apartments for rent. I started to fantasize about us working on the same street. Maybe we could meet up after work and have coffee. Or I could go to her apartment to unwind after a long hard day at O'Malley's diner. Maybe now we could start to build a normal, healthy relationship. Maybe she'd make me tea and I could complain to her about my love life. Maybe I'd end up moving in with her for a while, before moving to LA…

I allowed myself to fantasize about the ideal sibling relationship I never had, but always wanted.

We started apartment hunting. Well, *I* started apartment hunting. I searched Craigslist, contacted landlords and potential roommates, and set up appointments. With Sibby in tow, I walked in ahead of her to each interview, prepared to take the lead, lest my unpredictable sister say something to cost her the opportunity.

We looked at a single on Ferry street. One spacious room on the second floor, with a kitchen. A large window with venetian blinds looked down on the popular crack-dealing side street below.

"I'm just scared of you living alone on this street," I confided in a whisper, so the large Russian landlord in a wifebeater wouldn't hear.

"I know. Me too," she agreed.

We stopped at O'Malley's for lunch. Connor, the diner's owner, came over to say hello. "We're apartment hunting for Sibby," I told my boss. "But, honestly, I'm a little afraid for her safety in this part of town." The north end of Main Street was a notoriously dangerous part of Middletown.

"Donnie lives on Ferry Street. He'll watch out for her," Connor said.

Donnie, hearing his name, came over. Donnie was Connor's girlfriend's son: a kind-hearted beer-guzzler who worked at the diner whenever he had his shit together. His brief stints of employment were eventually interrupted by drinking binges where Connor would have no choice but to fire him. But he always hired him back when Donnie teetered back to a functional level of alcohol consumption.

Our mother used to party with Donnie. She also worked at O'Malley's once in a while, and had found herself a drinking buddy. I had gone out to the pool in Gumma's backyard one day to find Denise and Donnie swigging brewskis on the deck. They seemed embarrassed I'd caught them. As if they were teenagers disobeying the rules, and I the mother.

But despite his substance abuse, Donnie was a good guy. I knew he would look out for my sister, and that he had the street cred to ward off any potential ne'er-do-wells.

"You don't have anything to worry about, Siobhan," he reassured her. "You'll be safe as long as I live nearby."

Thank God for my diner family. They would help take care of my sister.

We settled on an apartment a few blocks south of Ferry Street with a Serbian male roommate. The small dwelling had a kitchen, shared bathroom, tiny living room and two bedrooms. It was a steal at two hundred and fifty dollars a month. I was confident anyone could earn that and have money left over for bills and living expenses. I guess I momentarily forgot I wasn't trying to help just anyone.

I paid her first month's rent and half a month for a deposit with my own money, happy to help my sister begin this new chapter in her life.

Then off we went to find her a job.

Voicemails from My Sister

"Let's head out on foot. Ideally you'll work as close to your apartment as possible, since you'll be walking," I began.

Sibby was getting restless.

Oh no, I thought. *Don't turn ungrateful on me now. We're on a roll.*

The first business we scouted was Ferraro's, an old family-run toy store that had been on Main Street forever. "It'd be cool to work here, Sibs," I said. "You could play with all the toys." I asked the cashier for an application. Stepping over to the side counter, I watched Sibby slowly start to fill in the page. Her handwriting looked like a first graders. Even the way she held the pen was child-like.

"Here, I can fill it out for you," I offered. "I'll be faster."

She didn't argue, but seemed deep in her own head. Down the rabbit hole she was falling into a triggered state. I could tell by her silence.

We handed in the paperwork and I made the call.

"Let's quit for today. We can job hunt again tomorrow," I said.

I drove her back to her hoodlum friend's house in silence.

The next day I made good on my promise, picked up a now-rested Sibby, and took her hunting again for the perfect first real job.

All day we filled out applications: Dunkin' Donuts, Baskin Robbins, Subway, Record Express, Pelton's Drug and the Destinta movie theatre. When the sun began to set, we moved a few boxes into her new apartment so she could spend her first night there. Thankfully, her room came with a mattress and box spring (a huge selling point), so I made her bed and prepared to leave.

"I'll be here tomorrow at nine so we can go get the rest of your stuff."

She looked scared.

"What's the matter?" I asked, somewhat impatiently. I had done for her all day and was quite ready for some quality me time in my own home.

"Nothing. Just forget it," she muttered.

The next morning I arrived at nine on the dot. Sibby's roommate, Goran, let me in. Sibby was awkwardly traipsing around the kitchen making toast. Goran was boiling water on the stove for tea. Neither one seemed comfortable in the other's presence yet, but I dismissed this as the normal getting-to-know-you phase.

Sibby and I began our drive to Woodbury Circle to retrieve the rest of her things from her good-hearted creature-of-the-night friend's house.

"How was the first night in your new apartment?" I asked eagerly.

"It was OK," she murmured.

I felt her discomfort. "It'll get better, Sibby. It takes time to get used to a new place."

She nodded, but remained silent.

Voicemails from My Sister

When we got back to her apartment with a carload of suitcases and boxes, Goran had a message for Sibby. "Subway called. They want to know if you can come in for an interview tomorrow."

"Sibby, that's so great! Call them back, right now," I said enthusiastically.

I listened as she scheduled a meeting with the manager for the following day at four p.m.

After my diner shift the next day, I picked her up. I sat at an adjacent table at Subway just far enough away so that I could eavesdrop on her interview. She was professional and the most likable version of herself. After fifteen minutes, the manager concluded the meeting by telling Sibby that she'd like to bring her in again the following day around the same time to meet the general manager. Sibby glanced over her shoulder at me, to silently ask if I could drive her. I gave the thumbs-up.

So, after work again the next day I retrieved my sister to take her to her final interview. When I entered her room I saw that she was dressed too casually for this important meeting. Wide-leg jeans and a too-small polyester printed shirt made her look like she was going to a rave in someone's garage instead of a job interview.

"Here, wear this." I handed her a white button-down. "Do you have any black pants?"

She changed and we went on our way.

I stayed in the car for her second interview to give her her privacy. Afterward, we headed to Denise's house to retrieve more of Sibby's possessions to move into her new place.

After we chatted about how well her second interview had gone, she broached a new subject. "What do you think about me moving to New York?"

I almost slammed on the brakes.

"What!?! What the fuck are you talking about? We just got you a new place and you're thisclose to getting a job!"

She was unfazed. In fact, this dynamic was where Sibby was most comfortable. Me freaking out meant she could remain calm. She liked the shift in power. *I* was the one who usually wore the pants. She enjoyed snatching the rug out from under me.

"I was talking to my friend Toby who lives in New York and he said I could stay with him for a while and work in his Halloween store."

"It's March!" I exclaimed. *What the hell is happening here? I just spent all this time, energy and money helping Sibby get on her feet and now she just wants to piss is all away!*

"Sibby, if you up and leave now, after all I've done for you, don't ever ask me for help again. I will never bend over backwards to help you again."

"OK," she replied calmly.

We continued driving in silence.

The next day she was hired at Subway, and we finished moving all of her belongings into her new space.

Voicemails from My Sister

Two days later she moved to New York. Abandoning her stuff, she left with only fifty dollars in cash and a backpack of clothes.

"I'm so sorry about this," I apologized to Goran. He was extremely forgiving. I think he saw it coming. He refunded me the security deposit of one hundred and twenty-five dollars, but kept one month's rent. I collected Sibby's things and brought them to Denise's.

"It was good of you to try to help," my mother complimented. "But Sibby's just unpredictable."

I'd meant what I said. I would never help my ungrateful sibling again.

Nine months passed. Then she called. She had been couch-surfing in the city, but had exhausted her resources and needed to come home.

"I told you I'd help you once, but you took off, so I'm not helping you again." I held firm.

My father echoed my sentiments. "You can't come back here," he said angrily.

Sibby moved back to Connecticut and in with our mother for the next 2 years while waiting to be approved for Section 8 housing and Disability.

In 2006 she moved into a one-room, 175-square foot apartment. She gathered her things from Denise's and began her life of living off state assistance.

Chapter 10
Ward of the State

When Siobhan was granted Social Security Disability and Section 8 housing, the process mandated the signing of her rights over to the care of the state of Connecticut. So, as their ward, she was required to be evaluated by a state psychologist. At nineteen years old, Siobhan was diagnosed with bipolar and schizoaffective disorder and put on a heavy cocktail of psychiatric medications. She had to remain in a therapeutic state, you see. Tame, calm, subdued.

Psych meds were not new for Sibby. She'd been on Ritalin for years. But now her dosage was upped and other meds were added to strengthen the effect.

A nurse came to her apartment every morning to give Sibby her daily pills. Sometimes they'd watch her take the first dose, other times Sibby would scream at them so they'd just leave. Sibby may or may not take her medicine that morning. God only knows if she *ever* took her nighttime pills. My guess is she did not.

Nothing ever "worked" for Sibby. She remained unhinged, combative, delusional. She met with a therapist once every two weeks for talk therapy. She saw a psychiatrist every three to six months for medication review. Sometimes they'd rearrange the combination of pills that she was supposed to be taking, adding the newest drug on the market, subtracting the most expensive pill. Risperdal, Seroquel, Abilify, Clozapine, Thorazine, just to name a few. She took them all, inconsistently and in various doses. She hated taking her medicine because she said it dulled her.

Voicemails from My Sister

The insanity continued.

Chapter 11
Sibby's Resume

Here's the thing about having multiple psychiatric disorders: you can't really hold a job.

In 1998, when Sibby was fourteen years old, she was hired at Lyman Orchard's haunted corn maze. The man-made maze, where patrons were scared by costumed actors who'd jump out at them, was staffed mostly by high schoolers. It was a three-weekend-long stint, and Sibby loved it. She inserted her fangs, painted her face white, and donned her cape, alternating between the role of a vampire and a tour guide. This remains the one job she saw all the way through without getting fired or ghosting. (Pun intended).

The following year my friend offered her a part-time summer gig at his printing company. She'd simply have to make copies and answer the phones at this family-owned business. But after one shift, Sibby announced she couldn't get a ride to Hartford anymore, so she had to quit. This after insisting she *could* reliably transport herself to and fro only a few days earlier, when begging for the job.

Our father, a workaholic, always insisted that Siobhan work. After all, *I* had begun working at fourteen, so why the hell couldn't she? It was time she learned some responsibility, God dammit!

At 17 she got a job as a counter person at Mamoun's restaurant on Main Street. Wanting to support her, I went in to eat. She looked miserable. Ringing up my order seemed to cause her more stress than she could handle, and she looked ready to cry. Luckily no one else was in the small eatery. I took a seat and waited for my food.

"Siobhan, sweep the floor, please," her manager instructed. I watched out of the corner of my eye as she fought with the broom, moving it around the floor in circles as if it were a mop.

"Sibby, you have to sweep in a straight line," I whispered, attempted to help.

"Stop bitching at me!" she shouted back. She was on the verge of a panic attack. Not wanting to provoke a scene, I finished my meal in silence.

A week later she stopped showing up to that job.

"You want money, get a job," our father retorted when Sibby informed him that she needed twenty dollars for a field trip.

That summer she got hired at CVS, where she maintained employment for four months. It is the longest period of consistent employment she's ever held. The drugstore was within walking distance of our father's house, so when she couldn't get a ride she'd huff it along the busy, sidewalk-less street. She occasionally acted as a cashier, but after a few awkward encounters with customers her manager reassigned her to "go backs" and "facing" duties that did not require her to interact with the public.

In 2002 she became an Avon lady. Wanting to support her new endeavor, I bought $100 worth of goods. It was her only sale. A few months later she received a letter from a collections agency because she'd never paid Avon their 70%. The money was long gone, so she ignored the bill and promptly forgot about it.

In 2004 she was hired and fired from McDonald's the same day. After smiling her way through her final interview, the general manager shook her hand and welcomed her aboard. Sibby, who had a habit of getting too comfortable too quickly, promptly began telling the GM a personal story about how her last boss had pissed her off so she told him to go fuck himself. After a brief beat of awkward silence, he took back his uniform and informed my sister that this wasn't going to work out after all.

Sibby decided she was an entrepreneur in 2011 and began making beaded bracelets with the intention of selling them on eBay and at flea markets. But as usual she couldn't get rides to flea markets, or booths were too expensive, or she couldn't get rides to the post office to ship out her sales, so she wound up in the red with more merchandise than she could ever possibly hope to unload.

"I've been babysitting recently," she informed me in 2012 in one of our tense phone calls. *Good God, who would trust her with their kid?* I worried. Turns out it was one of her ne'er-do-well friends and she was watching their kid for free.

In 2020, at age thirty-six, after a sixteen-year employment gap, McDonald's hired her again... She didn't even make it to her first shift.

"I'll get another job." She sounded so sure. She lived so deep down the rabbit hole of denial at this point. I didn't argue.

Chapter 12
The End of Make Believe

It was a warm summer day in 1989. My sister was five and I was ten. We were playing dress-up downstairs at 145 Bend Lane, the four-bedroom farmhouse we'd just moved into next door to our grandparents, Gumma and Da. Sibby had on a long purple skirt over her stretch pants, and a flowing, sheer, floral button-down over her tee shirt. Her hair was stuffed messily under a kerchief, and she wore an arm full of jingly bangle bracelets.

We were making believe we were gypsies on a pirate ship. The front door was open and we utilized the entire downstairs and front porch as the setting of our "ship." Our mother was doing chores upstairs, so she turned up CNBC on the living room TV as loud as it would go so she could hear it. Being the creatives that we were, Sibby and I integrated the noise as part of our pirate atmosphere. A passing ship full of pirates, or what have you. Deck noise, you know?

We were mid-scene. I called to my sister from the kitchen to bring me a sword. She did not respond. I entered the dining room and called out again. Still nothing. As I entered the living room, I saw her standing directly in front of the blaring TV screen, unmoving. How dare she abandon our game for a TV break!

"Sibby!" I yelled and grabbed her by the arm. "Come on!" I said.

I turned to lead her away from the noisy box, but her body was unresponsive and she fell, limp like a rag doll, onto the floor.

Voicemails from My Sister

"Mom!" I screamed in fear.

Running down the stairs, my mother saw my sister lying on her back, her eyes open but unblinking, like a zombie.

"Oh my God!" She freaked out. "She's having a seizure!"

I don't know how she knew this. To my knowledge, my sister had never had a seizure before. She picked her up in the cradle position and ran out the front door.

"Grab my purse and keys!" she yelled back at me.

Crying, I hurriedly obeyed. What was happening? We were just playing dress-up two minutes ago! Was my sister dying?

"Oh God, she's foaming at the mouth!" my mother updated me as I ran after her. She threw her in the passenger seat. "Kate, you stay here."

"No! I want to go!" I pleaded, afraid this might be the last time I'd see my sister alive.

"I can't leave the house open! Stay here!" she screamed as she started the car and peeled out of the driveway.

I cried as I walked back inside. I shut the front door and turned off the TV.

Ever the mother, I thought, *what needs to be done now?*

I called my dad at work.

"Sibby had a seizure. Mom just took her to the emergency room. It was so scary, Daddy!"

Voicemails from My Sister

"Holy shit," my dad replied. He sighed a deep, contemplative sigh, as if trying to decide what to do next. "It's gonna be ok, honey. You just be strong. Call me back as soon as you know anything. I love you."

My father's words soothed me. If he said everything was gonna be ok then everything was gonna be ok.

I changed out of my costume.

The phone rang. It was my mother.

"Sibby's ok. They're gonna run some tests. Did you call your dad?" I told her that I had called my dad and grandmother, Gumma. I did NOT tell her that I had also called *her* parents, Nana and Papa.

"I'm coming home to get you."

Ten minutes later my mother barreled through the door and immediately poured herself a vodka tonic. She chugged it as she dialed my father, and chased it with another as she gave him the details. A few minutes later we headed to Middlesex Hospital.

My mother had calmed down now that she'd had her liquid relaxer, and she chewed her cheek in contemplative silence as she drove.

"What were you two doing, anyway?" Her tone was accusatory.

"Nothing," I automatically, defensively replied. "We were just playing dress-up."

Of course she was looking for a way to blame this on me. No way could she accept responsibility. I was only ten years old and even *I* knew that Sibby should anticipate some health problems after being fed alcohol and cocaine in the womb.

We drove the rest of the way in silence.

My sister's tests revealed that she had epilepsy. She was prescribed an anti-seizure medication and released.

The next afternoon I called Nana from Gumma's house, where I wouldn't have to hide the call, to let her know that Sibby was ok. I thought of the letter that Nana had shown me years before, which had been opened, then marked, "Return to Sender," and returned.

8-18-85
Dear Denise:

Dad and I are returning the check you wrote us because we feel you cannot afford it and we do not need it. You were in no condition to know how much you had spent on the weekend and I am sure you need the money for more important things.

I think you should know that you were so drunk that you jeopardized both children's lives by putting them in your car and attempting to drive when you could not even see. You asked me to clean your glasses when it was your eyes that were foggy. You told Kate that if she got out of the car you would MURDER her. I think you should seek help and be very careful of how you handle the children because Kate is so sensitive that she could have very serious emotional problems if things go on this way. She is only six and not responsible for the care of her sister.

Screaming only makes the situation worse. Kate and Siobhan are both babies in a sense and "minor infractions" are to be expected. I hope you will be careful in the future not to repeat the scene you made here at any other place. The neighbors sure got an earful.

Love to you all,
Mom

We hadn't been allowed to see my Nana and Papa since my mother got that letter. Denise's defenses shot up when she read it, which should've been a sign that there was some truth in it that she was not ready to handle. Instead of swallowing her pride and admitting she needed help, Denise had returned the letter and cut her parents out of our lives.

And now, her youngest child was diagnosed with a disease which she may have contributed to with her using. Her drinking, and now her denial, had to deepen in order to allow her to go on without looking at her problems.

"I miss you, Nana," I said into the phone.

"I miss you too, sweetheart. But hopefully someday your mother will choose to get help and we'll be able to see each other again."

Siobhan was prescribed Depakote, an anticonvulsant, which treats bipolar disorder and epilepsy. Since then she has only suffered one additional seizure.

Chapter 13
Michael

The week after Sibby's first seizure our mother tried to kill herself. I say she "tried" because, if you ask me, it wasn't a genuine attempt, it was just another cry for attention. As usual, she put minimal effort into the endeavor.

It was on this night that I met Siobhan's real father. I hadn't known Sibby wasn't Ed's biological daughter until I met Michael, the man who claimed to be her daddy, as he screamed at Denise to try and throw up the bottle of pills she'd swallowed.

"Hi Kate, I'm Siobhan's father," he introduced himself, far too casually, given the circumstances.

Traumatizing news had a nominal effect on me at this point. I had a very high tolerance. Ten years of absorbing disturbing information resulted in diminished impact.

"OK, what's going on?" I asked.

"Your mother wants to die," he answered nonchalantly.

Awesome. That's what I wanted too.

Michael edged closer to me and I could smell vodka on his breath. He and Denise had been partying together, right downstairs from where Sibby and I slept. My father was still on the road and our mother used his absence as an excuse to get wasted with, and possibly fuck, other men.

So, this was Sibby's DNA. Two licentious addicts.

Voicemails from My Sister

I studied Michael. He was moderately attractive, with light brown hair and eyes. He appeared lower-middle class; working class. But one feature stood out and verified that he was indeed my sister's papa — his nose. Sibby had his bulbous schnoz, alright. I sighed. *Well, OK. My sister is actually only my half sister.* I wondered if my father knew.

Years later I found out that both Eddie *and* Sibby had known that Michael was Siobhan's biological father. I have to hand it to my father for continuing to play the part of Sibby's dad despite knowing she wasn't his. It wasn't like him to take care of other people's stuff. Hell, it wasn't like him to take care of his own stuff either, for that matter.

Michael died when he was forty-nine years old. The same age that our mother died.

"You'll definitely live longer than me," Sibby said to me years later.

"What makes you say that?"

"Both my parents died young, so I have a short life expectancy."

I felt bad for her.

Michael had three other children with a different woman: one girl and two boys. Sibby believed that being blood relatives meant an automatic bond, so she'd gotten to know these half siblings through Facebook, and in 2014 she planned to visit Alabama to meet them.

Carrie, Sibby's half sister, was nineteen years old and pregnant with her third child. She was unemployed, on welfare, and had recently broken up with her abusive fiancée, Micky. Sibby, in true Al-anon fashion, vowed to help her sister/new best friend get her life back together again. Never mind that Sibby's life was out of order. She was determined to "be there" for her sister who "needed her."

I sent Siobhan money for a Greyhound bus ticket from Connecticut to Alabama. A plane ticket wouldn't've cost much more, but at this particular point in Siobhan's life she was terrified of the sky and refused to fly.

Siobhan arrived at the Livingston bus terminal and called Carrie from the pay phone.

"Can you hitch a ride here?" her frazzled half sibling allegedly begged. "Micky stole the truck, so I can't pick you up."

Being a people-pleaser, Sibby smiled and said, "no problem," into the phone, before walking the mile to her half sister's trailer, schlepping her heavy suitcases behind her. What had Sibby packed that weighed down the case, you ask? Two Nintendos to give to her nieces and nephews. "One is broken, but it's for parts, ya know?" she explained to her confused half family.

Siobhan, tired, dirty and hungry, arrived at Carrie's mobile home after dark. "Can I have some water?" she begged. Carrie, a baby glued to her hip, another swarming around her legs, filled a glass from the tap. Sibby chugged it, ignoring its recycled taste. (Later on she got diarrhea, which is an awful ailment to have in a mobile home, where the door to the bathroom is literally made out of paper.)

"Can I take a shower?" Siobhan tentatively asked.

Voicemails from My Sister

"Yeah, but we don't have any hot water right now," Carrie answered, as if it was nothing.

Siobhan hosed herself off in the shower that doubled as a toilet. They didn't have any soap, either.

Determined to help Carrie and her kids, Sibby assumed her role of oldest sibling and caring aunt. The following day Butch and Carson, Sibby's half brothers, arrived to meet her. Butch, the oldest of the three, was twenty-five, single, childless, and worked at a gas station. Carson was twenty-one and a father of two. He worked for the town of Livingston as a painter. All three siblings lived in Sutter trailer park. "Let's take the kids to the park so Carrie can take a nap," Sibby offered. The troupe rode in the bed of Butch's pickup to the run-down playground a half mile away.

"Be careful," Sibby singsonged to Buck, Carrie's three-year-old, as she pushed the baby on the swing. Playing the part of involved family member came naturally to Sibby. Underneath her mental illness was a beautiful, maternal soul.

But as the days of her trip passed, her affliction revealed itself. Without a nurse to force it down her throat, Sibby simply stopped taking her prescriptions. The result was messy.

On day two Sibby's bipolar schizoaffective disorder manifested as impatience. "Leave your kid alone!" she snapped at Carrie, who had grabbed a lighter out of her child's hand. "He's just a kid, for God's sake, you don't have to snatch shit from him!"

On day three Sibby began recounting false memories: "When I was five my mom and our dad took me to Disney World. Michael told your mom that he was going on a business trip, but he actually met us in Florida for a week." The three full siblings exchanged questioning looks, raising their eyebrows in suspicion.

On day four Sibby's rage appeared. "I need my cable, goddammit! Shifty's being interviewed on a talk show!"

"We don't have cable, Siobhan," Carrie replied impatiently.

"Jesus fucking Christ! Who the fuck doesn't have cable? It's a necessity!" She stomped outside to call me.

"Sibby, calm down," I attempted to quell her anger. "You're a guest in your sister's home. Be polite."

"No! Fuck her! She doesn't even get basic TV, Punkie!"

I asked to speak to Carrie.

"Your sister's crazy," she informed me. I sighed. I wondered if Sibby would make it four more days.

That night Siobhan went to Butch's trailer to crash on his couch. Luckily he had pot, which calmed Sibby down, but exacerbated her delusions.

"Michael tried to kidnap me when I was five." For some reason, many of her memories took place when she was five. "I never told anyone, but he came to my window one night while I was sleeping and said he wanted to take me to live with him and his new baby. That was you. Your mom didn't know he came. I thought about it, but then said no, I couldn't leave my family. They'd be too upset. He was disappointed, but he understood."

Butch was dumbfounded. He didn't know what to say.

Voicemails from My Sister

Sibby stayed with Butch for the rest of her trip, as Carrie no longer trusted her crazy half sibling with her children. She spent the remaining four days watching TV in Butch's trailer, smoking his pot, and telling him untrue stories. He was polite, but mostly remained silent, counting the minutes until she was scheduled to leave.

Once back in Connecticut and on her meds again, Sibby's brain rewrote the events of her trip. She called Carrie to thank her for a great vacation. "If you ever want to send the kids up here to visit I'd love to have them," she offered.

"Uh… no," Carrie responded, confused.

"Oh ok, well I was thinking, what if I moved down there? I could babysit while you go to work."

Carrie was stunned into silence. Didn't Sibby remember the chaos she'd caused? Why on Earth did she think Carrie would want her living there?

"Uh, I gotta go Siobhan. You take care."

"Oh OK, well, keep in touch," Sibby replied, dispirited.

They did not.

Chapter 14
Duck Muffin

Lyman Orchards is a quaint country store in Durham, Connecticut. There is an apple orchard where you can pick your own apples, and around Halloween they host the haunted corn maze where Sibby would work as a teenager.

One afternoon when Sibby actually was five, and I was ten, we went to Lyman's with our parents. They bought me a cheese Danish and my sister a banana nut muffin from the bakery, and we went outside to watch the ducks while my parents shopped.

There were an abundance of ducks in this duck pond. Seriously. It was way overpopulated. I think whoever was in charge of importing the ducks in the first place didn't realize ducks mate like rabbits, because there was barely any swimming room left. Because there were so many hungry water birds cohabiting, they had developed a ferocity when scavenging for food. These ducks, fattened by the bread of Lyman's customers, had become savage beasts, who viciously fought their own species for crumbs thrown by generous humans. If duck fighting were a sport, the fowl of Lyman Orchards would've held a title.

Sibby and I exited the store and headed for the benches surrounding the pond. I walked slowly, as all of my attention turned to devouring my cheese Danish. Sibby ran up ahead, over the small bank towards the ducks. Less than a minute later she was walking back towards me. I noticed she looked afraid and was sans delicious treat.

Voicemails from My Sister

"Where's your muffin?" I asked her, as I knew she couldn't have eaten it that fast. I was the chubby speed eater in the family, not my beanpole sister. Her eyes welled up with tears.

"Punkie, they were running towards me! Please don't tell Daddy!"

As I put two and two together, I started to laugh.

"Oh, Sibby! Come here!" I hugged her, my heart full of adoration. My poor baby sister! So eager to play with the cute ducks, who were only interested in her muffin. I could just picture the scene I had missed: adorable, smiling Sibby bouncing toward a flock of oversized mallards. Close enough to pet them, her grin turns to fear as it becomes evident this gaggle means to attack the holder of their dinner, who is roughly their same size. Sibby, fearing for her life, throws the food toward her predators, who then fight each other for it. Now afraid for the wrath of my father, who would scream at her for defending herself with the muffin he worked hard to be able to afford to buy her, she turned and attempted to walk nonchalantly, as if the near stampede hadn't just taken place. But her plan was foiled when I instantly called her out. She hadn't had time to build a solid backstory yet. Her fear was still fresh, her heart still racing. She was fragile, and broke instantly. The whole scene was so cute I just held her and laughed. Her fear began to diminish and she smiled and laughed with me.

"Come on, Sibby, let's go inside."

I led my sister back into the store, away from her assailants to safety. We found our parents, their cart filled with goodies: bread, cookies, Danishes, pies. You'd have thought they were carbo-loading before running a marathon, but no, they were just unable to do anything moderately. I was still smiling at the thought of my sister defending herself with a muffin against a gaggle of hungry ducks, while Sibby was still getting over it.

"What's going on?" my mother asked suspiciously.

"Sibby threw her muffin at the ducks!" I proudly announced. I couldn't keep it in. It was too cute and I knew my usually angry parents would get a kick out of it.

"What!?" my mother exclaimed, amused and curious to hear the full story. Sibby, seeing that my parents were having the opposite reaction to the one she feared, hurriedly explained. "They were all just running at me! I had to throw it!" My father laughed and put his arm around her.

"Aww Sibby, did the ducks try to eat you?" he cooed teasingly.

"Yes," she played back.

"Come on, let's get you another muffin."

We all walked back to the bakery together.

Chapter 15
Fishing

One day Ed, Denise and Sibby went fishing on Ed's small motorboat. Siobhan was around nine and she enjoyed bonding with our parents on the open water. Her favorite part was baiting the hook. My dad had a tackle box full of lures, but Sibby liked squishing a live worm onto a hook and watching it try to squirm off. I didn't like fishing or worms or bonding with our parents, so I stayed at Gumma and Da's that day.

After loading up Ed's rod, Sibby took a seat on the bench to watch. Ed prepared to cast his line. He reeled it in, then flicked it over his shoulder. But before he could fling it out onto the lake he heard a scream.

"AAAAAHHHHHHOOOOOOO!" cried Siobhan.

"OH MY GOD, ED!" Denise screamed, dropping her pole.

Our father spun around and saw his hook, with the worm still attached, stuck right in the top of his youngest daughter's head.

"Oh, shit!" Eddie dropped his pole and yanked the cord to motor up the boat, then sped back to shore.

Siobhan instinctively reached for the hook to pull it out.

"No! Don't touch it! The barb is in your head!" My mother freaked out.

Siobhan's sobs increased, but her hand slowly descended, and she left the lure sticking out of the top of her skull. The worm, still alive, wriggled on top of her head.

Blood started to trickle down Siobhan's face. Our mother used her shirt to wipe it away from her eyes.

Siobhan was shaking by the time they got to the truck. Denise loaded Sibby into the front seat while our father quickly pulled the boat out of the water and hitched it to the rear. Finally Eddie peeled out of the parking spot and barreled towards the highway.

Twenty minutes later the trio rushed into the emergency room. Heads turned to witness the shivering child with a hook in her head, still attached to the line and rod held by her father. It looked as if he had just fished her out of the lake.

An intake administrator ran out from behind her post and swept my family beyond the swinging doors to the ER, bypassing the group of people waiting to be admitted. This was a *real* emergency.

Our parents sat with Sibby, holding her hands on either side as a doctor injected her with lidocaine.

"We have to shave some hair," he informed the traumatized child. She began to cry again.

"Just a small patch. To make sure I get everything out, and that it doesn't get infected." Ed laughed, a slight scoff, as if thinking, *Jesus Christ, how could this possibly get any fucking worse,* but Sibby took it to mean that he'd hurt her on purpose, for his own amusement. Down the rabbit hole Sibby fell, further into self-pity and aloneness.

Voicemails from My Sister

The doctor was gentle and extracted the angle quickly without inflicting any more pain. Once the hook was out of her head Sibby stopped crying, and our parents relaxed.

The three stopped at Friendly's on the way to pick me up from Gumma and Da's, as if a butter pecan cone would make up for a hook in the head.

When they walked into my grandparents' kitchen my mouth dropped open in horror. Sibby's dark hair made the bald patch on top of her head stand out like a light shining from a tunnel. Her cheeks were strewn with tears, but she ate her ice cream cone with a manufactured smile plastered on her face. Her parents wanted her to be happy, Goddammit. I mean, come on. Enough crying already. It's done, over with. Eat your ice cream and quit whining!

My mother's expression suggested that she had a juicy story to share, wherein *she* was the victim. My father impatiently collected me. They both needed a drink.

Unhappily, we walked to our house next door.

Chapter 16
Basket Tossing

When Sibby was ten years old, Denise got some night shifts at one of her many short-lived waitressing gigs. I'd been living with my grandmother, Gumma, but occasionally visited my sister next door to "babysit" when my mother was gone for the evening. On this particular night, my best friend Erica was with me.

"Sibby, it's time to do your homework." I assumed the role of mother.

"No," she replied. She felt outnumbered because there were two of us, and antagonistic because we were in *her* house.

"Sibby, don't act up. Come on, go get your work."

Determined to rebel, she screamed, "NO!" and ran to her room, slamming the door behind her.

"Awk-ward," Erica singsonged. My miniature dachshund, Schuylar, emerged from the kitchen. He looked up at Erica, who looked down at him. Then he peed, maintaining eye contact with my friend the entire stream.

"Don't look at him, Goddammit!" The dog *always* peed when Erica looked at him. For some reason, Erica was like a diuretic, and Schuylar always lifted a leg and relieved himself when Erica glanced his way. She knew that. But it was too late. I scurried to the kitchen to grab paper towels and Erica burst into a fit of boisterous giggles, collapsing in an uncontrollable heap on the dining room floor.

Voicemails from My Sister

"STOP LAUGHING!" My sister's enraged voice bellowed from the top of the stairs. This random direction only exacerbated Erica's hysterics, and she regained her breath just in time to burst into another wild explosion of chuckles.

I ran to the bottom of the stairs as a laundry basket came flying down them, missing me and hitting the front door. Erica, on her back, grabbed her stomach, unable to breathe, and exhaled the loudest eruption of guffaws yet.

"GODDAMMIT STOP IT! STOP LAUGHING! STOP FUCKING LAUGHING!" my pubescent sibling repeated. The sound of Erica's joy infuriated her. She already felt ostracized, simply by us being there. The fact that we were having a good time only made her feel more alone. But the more she protested, the harder Erica laughed.

"Enough!" I had to put a stop to this crazy cycle. "Sibby, calm down!"

Erica caught her breath and sat up, wiping tears from her eyes. "You want us to leave?" I gave my sister back the power.

"Yes." Her eyes filled with tears. I don't think she really wanted us to leave. I think she wanted her anger to leave, but didn't know how to make it go away.

"Fine, we'll go. But do your homework."

"You're not my mother!" she spat, retreating back to her room.

Chapter 17
Alateen

In 1997, when she was thirteen years old, I took Sibby to her first Alateen meeting. Alateen, a branch of Al-anon, is a twelve-step support group specifically for teenagers of addicts. I'd been living with my grandmother, away from the nightly chaos of my drunk mother, for two years. Although I didn't see my sister all that often, when I did see her I noticed how nervous she was. For no reason, at all times, she was riddled with anxiety. Stick thin and prone to panic attacks, it was obvious that her progressive developmental disorders were being neglected by our worsening mother.

We sat in a circle in the attic of a church. The meeting was small and comprised of young people whose parents were mostly downstairs in AA. A box of donuts sat in the center of the circle. The leader began to read. Sibby reached for a donut. After the preamble, group sharing began. I nudged Siobhan to participate. She did so willingly, then reached for another sweet treat. Members of the group relaxed as they identified with each other; nods and "mms" of recognition increased and serenaded the shares. I felt like a good sister, as it seemed Siobhan was getting something out of this meeting. Then she reached for a third donut. "Sibby, no!" I exclaimed. "Jesus Christ, doesn't your mother feed you?" An awkward silent beat followed, and Sibby pulled her hand away.

After the meeting, we met our cousins, Elizabeth and Mary, at the Athenian diner. It was almost midnight and I was high on pot, which I had smoked in the car. "I think I'll have the meatloaf," Siobhan stated, as she closed her menu. The three of us older girls broke into hysterical laughter.

Voicemails from My Sister

"Siobhan, you're not having meatloaf," I heckled. "It's almost midnight and it's thirteen dollars!" She didn't have any money, of course, so it was up to me to foot the bill for this late night snack. Embarrassed, she ordered a small side of fries.

A few days later I visited 145 Bend Lane, where she was living with my mom. I'd been feeling guilty about denying Siobhan a midnight dinner so, out of curiosity, I opened the fridge. My jaw dropped. Two half-empty 2-liter bottles of coke, a stick of butter, and a fresh bottle of tonic water were all that filled the ice box. I opened the freezer. It was stocked to the brim with Celeste personal pizzas. *Oh my God,* I thought. *My poor sister!*

The neglect was worse than I'd thought.

Sibby continued to attend Alateen whenever she could get a ride. The following year she went to a weekend jamboree. My father dropped her off at the Ramada in Cromwell on Saturday morning and she spent the weekend bonding with other children of alcoholics. The kids were paired up in rooms of two, and Sibby made friends with her roommate Sheila, a twelve-year-old from Old Saybrook.

She called me from my father's cell phone on the drive home. "Punkie, the jamboree was so fun! I won *A Day at a Time* book in the raffle and we made love collages!"

I was so happy for her. She was finding solace through camaraderie with peers who sought healthy solutions to their trauma. Maybe everything would be OK after all.

Chapter 18
You Can't Trust Your Friends

Siobhan was eight years old when our family relocated to Oak Park, Illinois, for a year. Our parents separated and our father was given custody of me and my sister, while our mother moved into a small apartment above a bar in Chicago.

Our father, then a stagehand on the first national tour of *Miss Saigon,* worked two days and six nights a week. As usual, it was my job to take care of my sister while he was at work.

Oak Park was a safe, upper-class suburb. Kids rode bikes everywhere, the public schools provided excellent, advanced education, and crime was low.

Sibby and I both made lots of new friends in Oak Park, and we'd hang out in various combos every day and night.

One day my friend Tevin came over to meet me and Sibby before we made our way to the "mall," a main street of stores, restaurants, and a movie theatre.

"Your sister's cool," he complimented.

"Yeah, she is," I agreed.

I went into the bathroom to pee and fix my scrunchie before we left our duplex, then emerged ready to go. I opened my bedroom door to gather my sister and friend, and Tevin stood up quickly. A guilty look on his face, he turned red and stammered, "Uh, yeah, we're ready," then looked at my sister. She looked ready to cry.

Voicemails from My Sister

"What the hell is going on in here?" I accused, though the answer was obvious. Tevin had been molesting my sister.

"What the fuck are you doing?" I yelled, and pushed him.

"Nothing, nothing, I — I," he stuttered.

"Did you fucking touch her?" I accused.

Siobhan started to cry.

"GET THE FUCK OUT OF MY HOUSE!" I shrieked, shoving him towards the door.

"I'm sorry! Siobhan, I'm sorry! I didn't mean to —," I slammed the door in his face.

I ran back to my sister, who sat sobbing on my bed. Hugging her, I shushed away her tears and told her everything was going to be alright.

"What happened?" I asked, once she'd recovered enough to speak.

"He asked me to come in your room with him and then he shut the door. I sat on the bed and he said he thought I was pretty. Then he kissed me and tried to push me down on the bed. Then you came in."

Oh my God, I thought. *What might've happened if I had taken only a minute longer?*

"I am so sorry, Sibby! I will never speak to him again."

Voicemails from My Sister

It was all I knew how to do. Cut the perpetrator out of our lives. I didn't tell our parents, and neither did Sibby. They wouldn't have done anything anyway. I just gave Tevin the look of death when I passed him in the halls at school.

In 1997, when Sibby was thirteen, our parents finalized their divorce. Denise moved into the small house on Bixby Street that we'd grown up in, leaving my sister in the care of our absentee father in the large house at 145 Bend Lane. As usual, Ed "had to work" all the time, so Siobhan was left alone every night. For some reason, my father chose to commute to New York City every day — two hours each way. He'd leave before Sibby got home from school each day, and arrive back home after she was supposed to be in bed. Sibby was expected to fend for herself after school, just as she had been while in Denise's care.

It didn't take long for Ed to decide he didn't like being a single parent, and he pawned Siobhan off on another family. "Sibby's going to stay with Gwyn and Marco," he explained to me, after three months of living with just his youngest. He immediately defended this decision. "I come home from work and the heat's on 80, all the windows and doors are open and she's out galavanting with her delinquent friends!" I guess he'd expected her to raise herself. Since she was incapable, he paid family friends two hundred dollars a week to take her in and try to get her to behave.

Sibby had been friends with Juan Carlos since kindergarten, so our parents and his befriended each other by association. The Gonzales household was full, loving, and disciplined. The arrangement started out great. Sibby, happy to be away from our abusive father, embraced this new life of schedules and discipline. She and Gwyn became close, like an ideal mother-daughter duo. Soledad, Juan Carlos's sister, and her infant daughter Jasmine, lived in the condo as well, and Sibby loved playing older sister to the adorable baby. Sibby's truancy decreased and her grades improved, as Gwyn supervised her homework each night.

For several months everything seemed great, and things looked like they might just turn out well for Sibby. Maybe thirteen *wasn't* too late to reroute her misdirected brain. Maybe her behavior *could* be corrected, eventually leading to a self-sufficient life. Things were looking up.

One night around 1 a.m. Sibby went downstairs to the kitchen to get a banana, leaving the lights off so as not to wake anyone. She approached the fruit bowl for a late night snack.

"Boo!" Marco, standing in the dark kitchen alone, scared her.

"Ah!" Sibby exclaimed in a loud whisper. Although she hadn't been expecting anyone to be there, she felt safe in this home, so her reaction was more surprise than fear. Marco smiled and walked towards her out of the shadows.

"What are you doing down here?" she asked her childhood friend's father.

"What are *you* doing down here?" he playfully chided.

"I'm hungry. I was just getting a banana," she replied.

"Go ahead," he encouraged, gesturing towards the bowl.

Hesitantly, she took the piece of fruit, wondering what was wrong with Marco? He was acting weird.

He silently watched while she peeled the banana. Then she took a bite.

Voicemails from My Sister

"Is it good?" he inquired.

"Yeah, I love bananas," she answered, attempting to smooth out the strange energy.

He took another step towards her. "Do you like living here?" he asked.

"Yeah, I do," she assured him, although this awkward encounter was making her question if that were still true.

"Good. We like having you."

Siobhan nervously took another bite, wondering if Marco was drunk.

Siobhan took the rest of the banana out of its peel and moved to throw it away. The garbage can was behind Marco. He stepped to block her, so that their bodies were almost touching. Then, without hesitation, he reached into her shirt and cupped her left breast.

"I'm sorry! I'm so sorry!" He jerked his hand away and jumped back, as if he honestly didn't know what had overtaken him.

Siobhan stood, frozen, holding the banana peel in one hand, unable to finish chewing the fruit in her mouth. Her eyes filled with tears.

"Siobhan, I'm so sorry. I don't know why I did that! Please don't tell anyone!"

Too triggered to respond, Sibby threw away the banana peel, and walked upstairs.

Voicemails from My Sister

She lay awake, her eyes wide open all night. *Another man hurt you,* the traumatized part of her brain told her. *You can't trust anyone.*

At least he said he was sorry, the hopeful part of her brain responded. *And he really did seem sorry...* Survival techniques and coping mechanisms fought in her mind.

The following morning Sibby, full of fear, put off going downstairs as long as possible.

"Siobhan, it's time for school," Gwyn singsonged up the stairs.

She hoped Marco wouldn't be there.

But no such luck. There, in the kitchen, stood the whole family, ignorant of the trauma that had taken place in that very room the night before. Their obliviousness triggered Siobhan, and she felt even more alone. Marco looked at her. His eyes seemed to say, *I'm so sorry,* and *please don't tell anyone.*

Two days later she called me at college and told me exactly what had happened. My heart sank. Why couldn't anything go right for Sibby? "Are you gonna tell Dad?" I asked her. "I mean, you can't stay there and he'll want to know why."

"I'm scared," she admitted. But she told him anyway.

He picked her up the following day, thanking Gwyn for all that she'd done. Sibby wanted to come home, he lied. Marco was not home, and my father did not reveal that he'd molested his daughter to his wife. As usual, he let my sister down.

Chapter 19
Got God?

Sibby and I weren't raised with religion. "If you're interested, you can learn about different religions on your own when you're older," our mother, an angry Buddhist, told us. "Then you can make your own decision. I'm not going to force a religion on you." But the truth was she was just too lazy to teach us anything.

Gumma secretly had me baptized when I was a baby. Denise was livid when she found out. "How dare she go behind our backs like that!" She scolded Ed, as if it were his fault.

Gumma and I would get on our knees and pray on nights I slept over. The Lord's Prayer. I loved this tradition. I felt a spiritual connection. Because I was baptized? Because we prayed? Because I had faith? I don't know, but something outside of myself told me everything would be OK when my parents abused me. A strength from deep down inside warmed me, and hugged away my fear. That was my higher power.

Sibby didn't have that benefit. Her soul was doomed. No one baptized her or taught her to seek a spiritual force outside of herself for solace. She was destined to be lost.

So, imagine my surprise when, in 1999, Sibby told me she had been attending church. "I talk to the priest sometimes," she revealed to me. "I like it. He's really nice."

Voicemails from My Sister

I was flabbergasted. She went to church of her own accord? By herself? She must really need a higher power. Perhaps to make sense of this tumultuous life she'd been born into.

"Can I go with you?" I asked.

"Sure," she responded. She was unusually calm.

We drove to the St. Francis of Assisi church on Silver Street, where Sibby had been walking twice a week on her own. My heart raced as I parked the car in the almost-empty lot. *Why am I nervous?* I wondered. "It doesn't seem like anyone is here," I said to Sibby. It was a Tuesday afternoon.

"Father Anthony's always here," she replied, pointing to his parsonage. "He lives here."

We walked inside. The chapel was empty and the lights were dimmed. Sibby knocked on an office door. A few seconds later a priest, dressed in a cassock, opened the door.

"Hello Father," Sibby greeted the older man. "I was hoping you had some time to talk today."

I was sweating with anxiety.

"Of course, Siobhan," he replied, opening his door wider. "Please, come in."

He knew her name. She hadn't been lying. It occurred to me that *that* was why I had been so hesitant. I thought she had imagined these encounters.

"This is my sister, Kate," she introduced me.

"It's a pleasure to meet you, Kate." He shook my hand. "Please, sit down."

He directed us to two large mahogany chairs opposite his desk. He took a seat behind his workspace and folded his hands, prepared to listen.

"I've been doing better." Siobhan got right into it. "I've been taking my medicine and going to school. My parents and I aren't fighting as much."

Father Anthony nodded. "… Good," he said, eventually.

"But I still feel angry at them," Sibby continued, beginning to open up.

Is this like therapy? I wondered. I was still too shocked at this whole situation to speak.

"Have you been praying?" he inquired.

"Yes, I have. I pray every night," Sibby continued. "I pray for my father, and for my mom. For my sister," she looked at me, "and our grandmother."

He nodded.

"But I still feel angry." Sibby choked up with tears of frustration.

I put my arm around her shoulders to comfort her.

"It takes time to work through anger, Siobhan." Father Anthony spoke softly. "But you mustn't give up faith. With continued prayer, your anger will lessen."

Voicemails from My Sister

I finally felt compelled to speak. "It's true," I agreed.

"You have a good sister," he complimented.

"Yeah. I do," Sibby agreed.

We stayed in Father Anthony's office for an hour. Sibby did most of the talking. She cried, she laughed, she confided, she purged. I chimed in when I felt I had something helpful to contribute, but mostly I just listened, as did Father Anthony. I was in awe of this dynamic. Siobhan had called on this man for help and he had opened his door wide and given it to her. It was unlike any other relationship in her life. Love, with no expectations attached.

Once we were back in the car I commended and praised my sister. "I am so proud of you for doing this, Sibby. I am so, so happy you've started talking to Father Anthony. I think it will really help you in the long run."

"Thanks, Punkie," she replied. But she was distant. As quickly as the Holy Spirit had entered her, it had left, it seemed.

She never went back to church again.

Did being vulnerable trigger her mental illness, causing her to shut down? Did my approval of the situation rub her the wrong way, making her not want to return? Or did she just forget?

Chapter 20
Never Mix, Never Worry

Antipsychotic medications and street drugs don't mix.

I didn't know. I was just grateful my sister and I had finally found something in common — we both liked having our minds altered.

Siobhan was eighteen and living with my father in the large house at 145 Bend Lane. Ed was at work and Sibby and I were hanging out in the spacious farmhouse smoking pot. Because she hated being alone, and her friends were always looking for somewhere to land, my sister invited a motley crew of delinquent deadbeats over to join us. Upon arrival, one of the crew suggested we get some mushrooms. Hell yeah!

The four of us continued smoking my pot while we waited for our harder drugs to arrive, and I judgmentally wandered into my own head, questioning where Siobhan had found these drifters. Sean, a long-haired skater-type, minus the skateboard or skill, head-banged alone in the living room to the Hellfuck CD he'd brought. Pete, the laconic, shy soul who was taken advantage of by his "friends" because he had a car, was overweight and in love with my sister, who denied him nookie, but kept him around for rides. Derek, the scary friend, who wore a black trench coat and a mean gaze, reminded me of the school shooters in *Bowling for Columbine*.

As we smoked, the energy turned dark. Siobhan, feeling powerful because she was surrounded by her friends, became angry. Her resentment at my father rose and, in an act

Voicemails from My Sister

of rebellion against his house, she ran into the living room and cranked "Killing Christ" up to 10.

"Sibby, no!" I shouted over the noise, and turned it back down to 3. "Fuck Eddie," she spat, "I hope I break his fucking stereo!"

A pair of headlights turned into the driveway. Thank God, our drugs were here.

Alice in Chains, heavy on the bass, suddenly muted as the dealers turned off the ignition. Two goth vagrants exited the beat-up Geo Metro and approached the house. A boy who looked to be about eighteen walked, with a swagger I was pretty sure he hadn't earned, towards the back door; a beautiful girl with black-and-purple streaked hair and perfectly done black eyeliner tiptoed shyly behind him.

I didn't want two more vagabonds in my father's house. The slacker ratio was high enough.

"Hi Lily," Sibby greeted the girl.

"Oh!" she said softly, clearly surprised to see my sister. Her face turned red. "Hi."

"How are you?" Sibby continued, and it was clear these two had a history.

"Fine," Lily replied, her eyes darting around to the rest of the group, scanning to see if we could tell.

"I like your shirt," Sibby complimented, trying to put her at ease.

Voicemails from My Sister

"Thanks," Lily laughed nervously, then took a step back, hiding behind the man with the drugs.

He pulled a sandwich baggie filled with mushrooms out of his poncho and smacked it down on the island, as if to say, *Voila!*

"You wanted a quarter?" he confirmed. I handed him three twenty-dollar bills, trying to hurry this transaction along.

"Bye Siobhan," the shy girl said as they turned to leave. She was clearly relieved to be exiting this uncomfortable encounter.

My sister looked hurt. "Bye," she replied, crestfallen.

"Who was that?" I asked.

"Lily," she replied. "We used to date."

I grabbed the bag of drugs and began divvying it up. The five of us consumed our psychedelics hungrily, and continued to smoke pot while waiting for them to kick in. A half hour later we were tripping. But instead of relaxing into a fun experience, the animosity increased among the young'uns, and my anxiety rose.

Sibby and her friends became angrier, more combative. Derek joined Sean in the living room and proceeded to mosh to the death metal CD, jumping on the couch, using the La-Z-Boy as a springboard. Sibby laughed maniacally, encouraging this destructive behavior, and enjoying the demolition.

Shy Pete broke out of his shell once the psychotropics kicked in, and partook in the concert scenario by playing air guitar in the dining room. Sibby, deeply altered into a state of

Voicemails from My Sister

fury, which made her chaotically happy, smiled like the Joker. I fought against the mind-altering drugs to try and control the situation. *Why had I thought this was a good idea?*

For the next three hours I babysat the barely-legal troop. Keeping the music beneath disturbing-the-peace volume, I removed matches from hands unless they were lighting a cigarette, and kept people out of my father's bedroom. Once it seemed Pete was level enough to drive home, I bid the boys adieu, and monitored Siobhan until she seemed stable. Then I said goodnight and went next door to Gumma's.

A week and a half later Sibby and I did Ecstasy. So, no, I *hadn't* learned my lesson.

I was shooting a short video, in which I cast my sister as the lead and Sean, Pete, and Derek as minor characters. The story was about "me" crushing on a guy, and Siobhan broke my heart with her honest performance. I was floored by her natural acting ability.

The second night of shooting was reserved for Sibby's hobo friends, who participated begrudgingly. They didn't like work, and were less-than-thrilled about taking direction from me. Siobhan, encouraged by my declaration that her talent was Oscar-worthy, behaved professionally.

The first shot went off without a hitch. "One-take wonders!" I complimented Sean and Pete.

The next scene proved a tad more challenging.

"Can we do that again?" I asked Derek. "This time, just throw the line away."

Voicemails from My Sister

Annoyed, he did a second take. Since I knew that was the best I was gonna get out of him, I moved on.

After a scene and a half was "in the can," Sibby's misfit trio of friends became restless.

"Yo, I'm sick of this shit." Derek led the exodus. "I'm not tryin' to be no actor."

"Yeah, I'm hungry," Pete seconded.

Siobhan looked crushed.

"Guys, we're halfway done. Can't you just stick it out? Please?" I begged.

"Nah, yo! Fuck your stupid movie!" Derek took pleasure in ruining my creative venture. "We're out. Come on, ya'll." Pete followed Derek, but Sean protested.

"I'm gonna stay here, guys."

Siobhan and I looked at each other. Her disappointed expression told me she was sorry. Although I was let down by her friends, I did not hold her responsible, and felt the urge to try and cheer her up.

"You guys wanna get some E?" Sean proposed, as if reading my mind.

Forgetting about the riotous results of the last mind-bending trip we'd embarked on together, I replied, "Yeah!" in true drug-addict excitation.

Thirty minutes later the same trench-coated dealer from the week before rolled into my father's driveway. (This time, sans Sibby's ex-girlfriend.) I paid him for everyone's drugs and we swallowed our pills before he'd even put the cash in his pocket.

Another half hour later the three of us were rolling, and I was reminded of the chaos that'd erupted in this very location nine short days earlier.

Oh yeah, I thought. *Sibby and her friends are out of control on heavy drugs.*

Sean popped in Iron Maiden and restarted his solo mosh pit, while Siobhan danced rabidly. I attempted to extinguish the anarchy before it resulted in a visit from the po-po.

"Drink some water." I handed Sibby a glass, undertaking the role of mother as usual.

"NOOOOOOOOO!!!!!" she howled, then kicked over a speaker.

Oh shit, I thought. *She's way more out of her mind on "E" than on shrooms.* I tried to remember what mood-stabilizers Siobhan was currently taking. *Seroquel? Or is it Risperdal?*

She got on the dining room table. "I can fly!" she proclaimed. "I have superhuman powers, Goddammit! I am a demigod!"

Sibby jumped off the dining room table and rolled under the coffee table. "I'm in a box!" she shouted. She lay on her back, facing the underside of the wooden bench, as if buried alive. She began kicking and screaming, as if fighting her way out of a grave. "I'm in a box, I'm in a box, I'm in a box!" she repeated. Tears welled up in her eyes, and soon she was sobbing. In my altered state, I understood her words on a deeper level. She was trapped within her mentally ill mind.

Chapter 21
Vampire

Easily influenced and seeking acceptance and love, Sibby befriended the goth kids of her high school. She began dressing in fishnets, ripped shirts, and Doc Martin boots. She dyed her hair Manic Panic Fuschia Shock and wore black lipstick. And she became a vampire.

Her new friends were members of this group of wannabe blood-drinkers, so she hopped onboard, no questions asked, in order to not lose her new pals. She was tractable and they were accepting. Sucked into the world of Devil worshipping, Sibby embraced the pop culture of her new religion and all that came with it. *The Craft* became her new favorite movie, *Buffy* her TV show. She put *The Vampire Bible* on her Christmas list (which my father bought her because he got us what we asked for on holidays, as long as we were specific and got our lists to him on time. God forbid he do any actual parenting and question this new choice of reading material.) She painted her bedroom black, and began saving her shorn hair "to be buried with."

Since no one was ever home to protest, my sister began hosting satanic rituals in her room. Her new boyfriend, Mike, a veteran vampire, suggested that the meeting place needed to be made more official, and convinced her to draw a pentagram on the hardwood floor. So, without taking into consideration the consequences, Sibby took out a Sharpie and freehanded a five-pointed star onto the floor. Now they could effectively summon the demon spirits during their neo-pagan ceremonies.

Voicemails from My Sister

My father discovered the defaced floorboards the following day, and beat the shit out of Siobhan.

Her commitment to the cult deepened. The more estranged she felt from her blood relatives, the closer she felt to the devil worshippers.

In 2002 she attended an energy transference. "What the hell is that?" I asked her.

"It's a ceremony where one person gives another person all of their energy. It's really tiring, Punkie. It takes a lot of energy."

"It takes *all* of your energy," I corrected, jokingly. "What's the point of it?" I continued.

"It's a healing process," she explained.

She pulled out an envelope of 4x6's and I flipped through thirty-two images of the backs of people dressed in black, standing in a circle in a Radisson banquet hall. "This was at a hotel?" I laughed.

"Yeah, it was at the hotel in Cromwell where we used to go to the Thanksgiving buffet."

God, the irony.

"Who's taking these pictures?" I wondered aloud, as they were from a spectator's point of view.

"Pete," she replied.

"Oh Sibby, are you still using that poor boy?"

Voicemails from My Sister

"Yes," she automatically groaned. "He's the only person I know with a car."

Chapter 22
Six Flags

In 1998 my dad took me and Sibby to Six Flags for his birthday. I was home from college for the summer and Sibby had just fought her way through eighth grade. Bored and searching for thrills, my father suggested we visit the amusement park for a day filled with junk food and excitement.

The fifty-minute drive to Agawam was strained, as usual. Ed played Rush Limbaugh several decibels louder than was necessary, trying to get the authoritarian talk show host to penetrate my and Sibby's thick skulls. I sat smiling, like a triggered yes-man, silently pretending the noisy AM show wasn't causing me a headache, while Sibby, stone-faced, stared off into space in the backseat.

"Listen, listen," my dad interrupted the quiet. He farted, then exhaled. "Ahhh…"

We continued on in silence.

It was a muggy day in June and the park was packed with sweaty adventure-seekers. After resentfully paying the too-high-tab for all three of us, our petulant father hightailed it towards the rides, expecting us to keep up. We ran to appease him, while he ignored our efforts. "Hurry up!" He disguised his command with a slight singsong, acting the part of a hyper child. Skidding into place behind him in a long line, we spent the next hour looking everywhere but at him, in order to avoid conversation.

"Want some water, Sibby?" I asked my dehydrated sister.

"I don't drink water," she refuted, as if I should've already known that. Ed scoffed and turned his head, denying his youngest the attention she was clearly seeking.

"Whatever." I dismissed her too, taking a swig of Aquafina.

Finally, the three of us were strapped in next to each other on the Elevator, Six Flags' newest ride. My father sat between us girls and, as the free fall began to slowly inch up, Sibby remembered that she was terrified of heights. "Ohhh, boy," my father chided, poking Sibby's fear like a bully. "Ohhh, no! We're gonna fall!"

I laughed, unsure of what else to do, incapable of any reaction that wasn't perpetrator-pleasing. Siobhan squirmed and shifted in her seat, fighting the oncoming panic attack. The ride stopped at the top, one hundred and thirty feet in the air, allowing its participants a brief bird's-eye view of the park. Then, it dropped.

"AAAAAAAGGGGGGHHHHHHHHHH!!!!!!!" Siobhan screamed bloody murder, and burst into tears.

"OH, WHAT A RUSH!" Ed exhaled, his delivery sounding like a junkie who'd just shot up heroin. And, also like a drug-addict, he ignored the daughter to his right, who fought with the ride's chest straps, trying to free herself, and closed his eyes to enjoy his high.

The machine bounced up and down a few times close to the ground before shooting back up again, prompting another scream from Siobhan. My father laughed, most likely at the feeling produced in his chest from the sudden movement, but my terrified sister took it personally, thinking he was making fun of her fear. Down the rabbit hole into the feeling of isolation she began to tumble.

Voicemails from My Sister

When we finally got off the death trap Siobhan, bawling, fell to the ground, overcome. Passersby stopped. "Is she OK?" they asked, concerned.

"She's fine." My father diminished her feelings. "Come on Sibby, get up."

Trembling, she obeyed Ed's command. If she didn't, he'd pull her up, and she feared his hand.

Siobhan remained traumatized the rest of the day. Refusing to get on any more rides, she stood on the sidelines and waited, as my father and I rode without her. Deeply triggered into a state of helplessness, she drifted farther away from us.

Chapter 23
The Halloween Party

In 1999 I invited Sibby and her boyfriend, Brock, a fellow creature of the night, to Boston for a Halloween party. My six roommates and I were throwing a huge college bash in our apartment and, as Halloween was Sibby's favorite holiday, I assumed she'd have fun at our brouhaha.

My best friend Holly picked up Sibby and Brock in Middletown and drove them to Boston, repeatedly explaining over the two-hour drive that they were not allowed to smoke in her car. The trio arrived agitated. Siobhan and Brock lit up cigarettes as soon as they exited the vehicle, as Holly mumbled to me under her breath that I 'owed her one.'

As marijuana was my solution for everything, I lit up a joint and passed it to my sister and her man.

The mood relaxed, and we proceeded to get dressed for the party. It was "pimps and ho's" themed. Holly had bought a leopard print push-up bra, which she wore under a sheer top. I had an eighties-style mesh shirt that looked like Madonna's from "Lucky Star." I paired it with jean cutoffs over fishnets. Sibby wore a skintight leather bodysuit and fangs. Brock simply wore what he'd arrived in: a beige trench coat that made him look like a flasher.

The keg arrived and I poured my sister and her boyfriend beers.

"Everybody owes ten bucks for the keg," my roommate, Avery, charged. I handed him thirty bucks without even check-

Voicemails from My Sister

ing to see if Sibby or Brock had any money. I knew they didn't.

People started arriving and soon our five-bedroom residence was packed with costumed college students.

People yelled over the loud music and I saw Siobhan fight with her anxiety, trying to get it to go away so she could have a good time. Noisy situations made Siobhan nervous if she was not in control of them. For instance, a raucous house party full of *her* friends was fun, but a boisterous gathering of *my* peers stressed her out. I caught glimpses of her struggle throughout the night. She was wrestling with her mental illness.

As I always had weed and was constantly looking for someone to smoke it with, I had retreated to my room with a few friends from my acting class. Holly watched as we loaded my bong, and naively asked how it made us feel. I offered her a hit, but she refused. Just then a deafening roar resounded through the apartment, trumping the music and silencing the commotion.

"GET OUT! GET OUT!" I heard Avery scream. I opened my bedroom door. Avery was shoving Brock and Siobhan towards the exit. The rest of the party followed in support, determined to banish my sister and her boyfriend.

"What the hell is going on?" I demanded.

Carmella, Avery's girlfriend, was in tears. "He tried to rape me!" she accused.

His head hung in shame, Brock opened the door and exited, with my sister in tow.

Voicemails from My Sister

"I was in Avery's room and he came in and shut the door and locked it, then pushed me down on the bed and tried to get on top of me."

I wasn't quite sure I believed her. She sounded like she was exaggerating.

"Well, we can't just kick them out. They have nowhere to go," I tried to reason with the crowd.

"NO FUCKING WAY THAT ASSHOLE IS COMING BACK IN HERE!" Avery was drunk and livid. The rest of my roommates seconded his statement, while our guests nodded in agreement.

Goddammit, Sibby, I thought, *Why do you associate with such lowlifes?*

I went to look for them. They were outside the apartment, unsure of their next move. Brock looked remorseful, but Sibby had turned belligerent. "Fuck your fucking roommates," she spat. "He didn't even do anything to that bitch. She's lying!"

"Look Sibby, they won't let Brock back in the apartment, but I'm sure I can convince them to let you back in. You didn't do anything wrong, and I can't let you wander all over Boston in the cold all night."

"No, fuck those fucking people!" she said audaciously. I was begging, trying to reason with her, which made her feel like she held the power in the conversation. "I'm standing by my man!" She took his arm and marched off contumaciously.

I was frustrated, but also worried about my sister. Where would they sleep? *Let 'em sleep outside,* my intoxicated

Voicemails from My Sister

brain argued defiantly. *That's what Sibby gets for dating losers.*

The following morning she called me. "We slept at the train stop." Guilt overwhelmed me. I had let my sister sleep in the cold right outside our apartment. I felt like a terrible sister. But, then again, what choice did I have? History had proven that the more I argued with her, the more defiant she became. If I had tried to force her to stay inside, abandoning her perpetrating boyfriend, she would've fought with me until it escalated to a physical fight. So, I had let her go. And she chose to sleep outside. I couldn't blame myself. But I did.

Chapter 24
Creative Solutions

Siobhan is very... imaginative. Yes, she's delusional, but before all that she was simply inventive. Creative endeavors are a healthy way to channel energy, so I encouraged and supported Sibby's every artistic attempt.

When Sibby was five and I was ten, we lived in Chicago for a few short months while on tour with *Les Miz*. Our mother discovered Take One video, a new make-your-own-music-video service downtown. She took me and Sibby there one afternoon to record ourselves lip-synching and dancing to our favorite songs. I wore pink spandex and a bowler hat while I pretended to be Debbie Gibson singing "Electric Youth." Sibby embraced her fierce inner cat, snarling and scratching the air to Whitney Houston's "Queen of the Night." Lasers darted diagonally across the green screen behind us. A virtual background of psychedelic colors enveloped us in waves. Looking back, it was so tacky, but as kids in the 80's we loved it. We played those videos for all of our friends, showing off our impressive lip-synching skills. If the tape of me impersonating Deborah Gibson were to resurface now I'd be beyond embarrassed. Sibby, on the other hand, would still show hers with pride.

Sibby began writing poetry as a little girl. Short stanzas, as her A.D.D. distracted her from being able to complete long verses. "Star light, star bright, I'll bet you have a nice family." That one was my favorite. It said so much with so few words. She'd sit on my top bunk looking out the window at the stars, then talk to one. "How are you?" A crazy inner dialogue began with the celestial body, leading Sibby down the rabbit hole of self-pity and jealousy. The star probably lived in a

Voicemails from My Sister

happy, well-adjusted household. She recorded her feelings on paper and shared them with others.

When she was in high school Sibby participated in a few open mic poetry slams at an indie coffee shop in Middletown. She frequented this shop regularly, befriending other night people, and so felt comfortable bearing her soul at the microphone. I attended with Puck, my boyfriend at the time, and we purchased witch's brew coffee drinks and took a seat at a high top table. Whereas many of the other participants' poetry was too long, angsty and depressing, Sibby's was brief, hilarious and confused (or deep and uplifting, depending on how you looked at it.) "Once upon a time, my inner soul cried a river. I gave it a flower." She turned the page. Scattered applause broke out. Was that the whole thing? "Mirror mirror on the wall, do you see me?" When her litany of stanzas culminated, I gave her a standing ovation.

When our grandmother, Gumma, died, Sibby read some verses she had written at her funeral. My heart jumped into my chest as Sibby approached the pulpit. Her delusions had been active and her energy level catatonic, so I feared what may come out of her mouth and how it would sound. Thankfully she didn't embarrass anyone and recited a length-appropriate few paragraphs about her grandmother being the definition of grace.

I got a video camera for Christmas in 2000 and Sibby and her friend Lynn would borrow it and go exploring, a la *The Blair Witch Project.* They entered the water tower in back of our house near the deserted parking lot and recorded their trespassing. "Oohh, look at this." Siobhan beckoned the camera, as if she were hosting a documentary. Lynn hurried over and pointed the lens at Sibby's findings — a sleeping bag and backpack. An abandoned homeless encampment. If they'd been attacked, at least footage would've been found.

Voicemails from My Sister

One day Sibby's hilarious yet crazy brain came up with a fun episode pitch, which Lynn told me about years later. "Let's dress up like men and go to my mom's house." She and Lynn dug through Ed's wardrobe and picked out a couple of plaid button-downs and jean cut-off shorts. They stuffed pillows into the pants to make them fit, and tied them on with belts complete with bass belt buckles (yes, our father had *multiple* fish belt buckles). Laughing at their appearance, Sibby ran into her room and grabbed her black eyeliner. She scribbled a beard on Lynn's chin, and gave herself a goatee and mustache. Then they topped their outfits off with Red and White Sox baseball caps, and headed for the bus stop with my camcorder. People laughed good-heartedly at the teens as they recorded their bus ride to Denise's.

"My name is Ed and I like fishin'," Sibby impersonated in a low baritone.

"I'm —," Lynn started laughing, interrupting her improvisation. "I'm... I'm Peter, and I —" She broke down again. "I like boats."

Sibby caught the giggles too. When they arrived at Denise's house Sibby turned the camera to record our mother's reaction. "What the — ?," She smiled and laughed.

"We're here to fix your refrigerator, ma'am," Lynn began.

"Yeah, we heard it was running. We caught it." Sibby cracked herself up.

Sibby participated in various school and community theatre plays over the years. Bielfield, our elementary school, put on original plays performed by fifth graders. Sibby was in the chorus of *Be Smart, Don't Start,* an educational series of

Voicemails from My Sister

scenes about the dangers of drugs, alcohol, and smoking. Two years later in seventh grade, she was in the chorus of *Tom Sawyer.* She played a ghoul in *Jesus Christ Superstar* her freshman year of high school, in a community theatre production put on to raise money for a disabled child. My parents and I proudly watched her from the packed house; when she sang her one solo line I cried. Her boyfriend at the time, Jimmy, played Judas and he was outstanding. I was humbled and so proud of her for participating in such a beautiful creative project.

Sibby befriended Jonah, a thirteen-year-old gay dancer from the show. He could do the "Oops I Did it Again" dance from the music video and Sibby and I tried to follow his tutorial in our father's living room to no avail. We were not dancers, but we wanted to be.

Working for Avon inspired Sibby to try makeup artistry as a hobby. I let her paint my face numerous times over the years to practice. I can't say she ever mastered the skill, but I applauded her efforts.

Sibby began DJing on Waste Heap, a public access internet radio show, after graduating from her alternative high school. Her music was full of scratches and blips, due to improper care of her CDs, so it was a good thing this show didn't have any listeners. Still, every time I could, I tuned in when she was on.

"I love that you announced that it's Shirley Manson's birthday!" I complimented her after a show. "You should talk more. Your music fun facts are my favorite part!" (Although I loved her playlists too, which jumped from pop to death metal to children's songs, like a lyrical reflection of her scattered brain.)

Voicemails from My Sister

"Thanks. Did you hear me promote Connor's book?" The owner of O'Malley's diner, where I had worked for years, had written a cookbook.

"No, I didn't, but that's so sweet!" I replied.

"Yeah, I said the title and that it's available in bookstores. I even gave a preview of one of the recipes for French toast du jour." I felt a warmness in my chest. Sibby could be very kindhearted.

She started making beaded bracelets as a way to earn money after high school. If she had been able to get it together to sell these wares she probably could've charged at least five dollars per bracelet. They were that good. Her patterns were consistent, her color schemes flattering. Some pieces had charms, some were just beads. She sent me a bunch and, surprisingly, they remain intact. With her track record I'd've expected the elastic bands to have snapped by now, but no. I still wear them sometimes.

As a pursuant of work in the film industry, I sometimes think Sibby could've been hired as a creative consultant purely based on her knowledge and passion of kitsch art. "I certainly hope they did a good fucking job," she said regarding the upcoming *Jem and the Holograms* movie. "I hope they had Samantha Clark involved, because she was the original voice of Jem. I'm telling you, Kate, I should have been involved in this." As crazy as it sounds, I can actually picture this fantasy coming true. Sibby is so unique, I actually think she could be hired for her creativity. Unfortunately, her lack of reliability would inevitably get her canned.

Chapter 25
All Better?

I'd been living in Los Angeles for a little over a year and had only talked to Sibby a few times during that time. I didn't know how she was doing. It wasn't that I didn't care. I just couldn't stand how our phone calls would always escalate into screaming matches. We had no patience with each other, so I avoided communication.

In 2005, when Sibby was twenty years old, my boyfriend Austin and I went to Connecticut for Christmas. I was nervous to introduce him to my family. He was close to his mentally healthy siblings. I worried what he'd think of my unstable one.

"I'm at Derek's," Sibby explained when I called to tell her I was in town. She had been living with her boyfriend and his mother. "I'd love to see you, though, and meet your boyfriend."

Austin and I drove to the dilapidated condos in Woodbury Circle to retrieve my sister.

"Brace yourself," I warned Austin. "Sibby is not like your sisters. She's crazy."

We rounded the corner to find my sister and her white trash beau standing outside waiting for us. They kissed each other goodbye, and Derek, who usually dismissed me, waved to me as I pulled over.

Voicemails from My Sister

"You must be the man who makes my sister so happy," Sibby said charmingly. "I'm Siobhan. It's nice to finally meet you."

Hmm. She was much more cordial than usual.

We hugged and she didn't squeeze too hard.

"It's so good to see you, Sibby." I allowed myself to feel excited. "I've missed you!"

She got into the backseat and started comfortably talking to Austin. "So, how did you two meet?" she inquired. *Well, this is going well,* I noted. *She's making a positive first impression.*

"Hey," I decided impulsively, excited because things were going so well, "let's stop at Lyman Orchards to pick up a pie for Christmas. We can show Austin where you used to do the haunted corn maze!"

"Yeah!" Sibby agreed. "Austin, you're gonna love this place. They have a duck pond, and when I was little I threw my muffin at the ducks. Punkie, tell him the story."

She was remembering things accurately.

The thirty-minute drive to Lyman's flew by as Sibby and I took turns reminiscing. She seemed more lucid than ever. Nicer, more calm, happier.

I turned onto Reeds Gap road and found an empty parking lot. Lyman's had closed early for Christmas Eve.

"Awww, bummer," Sibby lamented. "It would've been nice to bring a dessert to Dad's. Our father loves sweets."

Voicemails from My Sister

We stopped at Friendly's for an early dinner before heading to my father's house.

"Your sister seems completely normal to me," Austin said when she excused herself to go to the restroom.

"I know!" I agreed. "Trust me, this is not how she normally acts."

Perhaps she was on her best behavior because she was meeting Austin for the first time. I was sure she would reveal her true colors once she was in the presence of our father.

But no. Sibby remained calm, cool, and collected as our father took us all out to a movie. Things were going so well that I was eager to prolong our visit.

"Do you want to stay overnight with us at the Inn at Middletown?" I offered. "We got a suite. You could sleep on the pull-out couch."

"Oh wow, really?" She couldn't believe I wanted to spend more time together. This was a first.

"Yeah, I want to spend as much time with you as possible because we're only here for three days."

Sibby called Derek to tell him she wouldn't be home that evening, and the three of us drove to the quaint hotel to check in.

I was eager to smoke pot, but worried about sharing the drug with Sibby. She was in such a good mood, would smoking ruin it? Would she become her neurotic, paranoid self? I decided to take a chance and rolled us a joint.

Voicemails from My Sister

The three of us smoked, continuing our amiable conversation. *Whew,* I thought. *Thank God the weed didn't make her crazy.*

Marijuana emboldened me. "Sibby, I have to say, I used to be worried about you. I was afraid you wouldn't be able to take care of yourself when you grew up. But after today, I'm not anymore. You have grown into a smart, funny, beautiful woman."

She took a beat.

"It's because I'm not on any medicine," she revealed. "I haven't taken any mood stabilizers or antipsychotics in about six months."

My jaw dropped. Wait a minute. You mean, this was my sister in her normal state? Unassisted by pharmaceuticals?

That meant the drugs that were prescribed to help her be her most useful self had actually been achieving the opposite.

"Woah. That's crazy," I said.

"I'm telling you, Kate, the medicine they had me on made me paranoid and tired. I've been so much better since I've been off everything."

"Why did they have you on drugs that didn't work for you for so long?" I inquired.

"Because I'm in a state-funded program, Kate. They say they have to keep me at a 'therapeutic level,' which means on a lot of drugs, so they can work with me. But I fought and final-

Voicemails from My Sister

ly got my psychiatrist to take me off everything because I told him it was making me worse."

I suddenly saw my sister's situation clearly. She had been overmedicated in an effort to keep her tame.

"Well, I'm so glad you finally got off that shit, then. Because you are doing great."

"Thanks Punkie. That means a lot."

The following morning Austin and I went to the complimentary breakfast that was included with our suite. We enjoyed lobster, steak and eggs in the cozy downstairs restaurant while Sibby slept in.

I saved half of my meal. "I'm gonna take this to Sibby," I told Austin. "She loves lobster."

We opened the door to our room at an inopportune moment. Sibby, in her tee shirt and undies, had just arisen from her slumber. "Ahh!" she exclaimed, quickly pulling on her jeans.

"Oh, sorry Sibs!" I laughed.

"Perfect timing!" she joked. In the past she would've been triggered by us seeing her in her unmentionables.

"We brought you some breakfast. Lobster and eggs!" I revealed.

"Oh wow, fancy! I would've been happy with a banana."

We got ready and headed to our father's, stopping at CVS on the way so Sibby could buy our dad a card and DVD as a

Christmas gift. I noted that she had her own money. She never had money before.

Mannheim Steamroller played on the stereo at our father's house. Gina, Gumma's live-in health-care worker, prepared a Christmas feast. Our father was in good spirits and smiling. It was like a fairy tale. I couldn't help but wait for the other shoe to drop, for holidays had never been without stress and anxiety in our house.

Our dad poured us mugs of spiced cider and we gathered in the living room to open gifts. "Are these new curtains?" Sibby asked.

"Gina made them," our father responded. "Aren't they nice?"

"Oh, wow. I'm impressed. They're beautiful," Sibby complimented. "Nice work." I noted that Sibby now gave praise readily. She never used to do that before either.

The morning continued perfectly. Sibby remained charming. Our father, convivial. We opened gifts slowly, appreciating each other's generosity, taking breaks to speak to extended family on the phone.

In the late afternoon we visited the Romanos, long-time friends of our family. Sibby remained charming and respectful in their home. In the past she would've acted out, as she felt uncomfortable in other people's environments.

Returning to our father's, it was now time to open our most extravagant presents. Our father always saved the biggest, most expensive gifts for last, increasing our excitement, knowing the best was yet to come.

Voicemails from My Sister

He handed Sibby a card. She opened it with care, so as not to tear the envelope. Inside was an oversized American Greetings Christmas card that read:

> *To My Daughter, I know I have a wonderful daughter because I see your strengths and talents, your warmth and thoughtfulness and the way you care about people. I see the person you are inside — the goodness and generosity — and I want you to know how much I love you and how grateful I'll always be to have you as my daughter. Merry Christmas.*

He signed the card:

> *I am so proud of the woman you've become, and so grateful to be spending Christmas with you. I love you. Love, Daddy*

A check for $2,000 fell out of the card. Sibby picked it up, absorbed the large number, and started to cry. Our father turned red with embarrassment. He'd expected gratitude, but not to this degree.

"Thank you so much," Sibby sobbed. This was a life-changing amount of money for her.

I went over and hugged her. Our father followed.

The next day I took Sibby to the bank to deposit her check. "Use this money wisely," I warned.

"I will," she promised.

We dropped Sibby off at Derek's house before heading to the airport to return to LA. "It was so nice to meet you," Austin said earnestly, as he hugged her goodbye.

Voicemails from My Sister

"Agreed. Welcome to our family," Sibby replied. I beamed with pride.

Silently I prayed that this better version of Siobhan would last. Because deep down, I knew it wouldn't.

Chapter 26
Gina & Tanesha

By the time Sibby turned twenty-one she was enveloped by mania. Like a yo-yo she fell into fiery pits of rage for no reason at all, then bounced back to a state of happiness as if nothing ever happened. I don't think she even remembered her moods from one minute to the next. She was temporarily living with our father again at 145 Bend Lane, after Derek's mother kicked her out. She and Derek had fought, the police had been called and now both she and Derek were filing restraining orders against each other. I suspected she must be back on her meds.

Gumma was nearing the end of her life, so my father stayed at her house part-time to take care of her, coming next door to the house he shared with Sibby only to sleep, shower and change.

Ed hired Gina, an illegal immigrant from Jamaica, to care for Gumma full-time. She moved into my old room in Gumma's house, where she lived for three years. She was kind, soft-spoken, and patient, even when Gumma called the police to report her as an intruder. Nothing fazed her. Eventually she became like a member of the family. She cooked delicious Caribbean meals and even sewed new curtains for the living room.

I felt bad for Gina, though, as her job was 24/7 and only paid $500/week. Most of the money she sent back to her mother and son in Jamaica.

"She has no overhead," my father argued. "All of her bills and food are taken care of."

Voicemails from My Sister

"I know," I replied. "I just think she must be lonely in that house all day."

My father eventually offered her use of the car and suggested she take some night courses at the community college, which was only a mile away. "Gumma can stay alone for an hour or two if you want to get out of the house. You should. It'd be good for you." But Gina didn't want that. She wanted an American man to marry her so her son could come to the US and they could become citizens.

Eventually my father and Gina started sleeping together. He had a girlfriend, Tanesha, who lived in NYC, but that didn't stop him. He was, by his own admission, scum.

Then it was like his twisted brain thought, *OK, now that I've successfully cheated, how do I make sure these broads find out about each other?*

Tanesha knew Gina as Gumma's live-in helper, though she'd never met her. Gina didn't even know Tanesha existed.

One day I got a phone call in LA from Gina, crying hysterically. He'd left an email from Tanesha open on his laptop on the kitchen table for Gina to find.

"Who is this woman, Tanesha?"

"Tanesha's his girlfriend of, like, three years or more. They work together."

You'd've thought I'd slapped Gina. Her sobs amplified.

Christ Ed, I thought. *Why are you so fucked up?*

Voicemails from My Sister

I pictured his sick mind planning how to get Tanesha find out about Gina next.

That night Ed lied to Gina, diminishing his relationship with Tanesha, and got her to forgive him. He invited her to sleep over 145, leaving Gumma alone in the house next door. The next morning, as if choreographed by our sick father, Sibby caught Gina exiting our father's bedroom.

"Oh! Uh… hi," Sibby stuttered, surprised to see Gumma's aide at her house.

Gina smiled to put her (hopefully) future stepdaughter at ease. "Good morning, Siobhan. Want me to make you breakfast?"

Because Sibby couldn't keep a secret (and our father knew that) she called Tanesha later that day. "This morning I saw Gina coming out of Ed's room in her underwear," she revealed.

Tanesha called me in LA, sobbing.

"Sibby, why did you tell her?" I scolded my nosy sibling on the phone.

"She had a right to know!" she shot back.

Our father continued boning Gina, and she tried to wear him down to get him to legally commit. Tanesha moved to the sidelines, but continued to be there for our father as a friend. Siobhan continued to battle manic anger, and a huge resentment against the new live-in girlfriend quickly formed.

"Where's my fucking Buffy DVD?" she screamed at Gina, while my father was at work. (She still wasn't ballsy enough to raise her voice in front of my dad. He would kick her ass for that shit no matter how old she was.)

"Siobhan, I haven't seen it," Gina calmly replied.

"You're full of shit. I know you took it!" Sibby accused.

"Sibby, calm down."

She called me in LA and told me what happened.

"Sibby, what the hell would Gina want with a Buffy the Vampire Slayer DVD? You lose everything. I'm sure it's just somewhere in your filthy room."

"No, fuck that slut, Punkie! She's trying to steal Dad away from us. She's using my stuff to get to him."

"You're insane."

A few days later Gina drove Sibby to Denise's. Gina was no longer just a live-in caretaker for Gumma, at this point. She had now become a full-time errand-runner and caretaker for Sibby and our father as well.

Siobhan was in a state of frenzied indignation. Not that anything had prompted it, mind you. She was simply jumpy at all times. She lit a cigarette to calm her nerves.

"Siobhan, open a window," Gina instructed.

"Fuck you, bitch! Just drive the fucking car!" Siobhan exploded.

"No! You can't talk to me like that!" Gina finally stood up for herself.

Voicemails from My Sister

"You can't tell me what to do! You're not my mother!" Sibby grabbed a handful of Gina's weave and yanked it out of her head.

"Oowwww!" Gina screamed, grasping her head with her hands. The car swerved into the other lane, tossing Sibby into the passenger-side door.

"Watch out, you crazy bitch!" Sibby shrieked, throwing the clump of hair out of the window, into the woods.

Gina slammed on the brakes. "Go get it! Go get my hair!"

Sibby smiled and calmly smoked her Marlboro. "No."

Gina broke into tears.

"I threw that bitch's weave out the window," Sibby bragged to me after relating the whole encounter later that day.

"Sibby, what's the matter with you? Gina is so nice and so good to Gumma. Why would you try to scare her away?"

"She's trying to get Dad to marry her, Punkie. I don't want that bitch for my stepmother."

There was no use trying to reason with Siobhan. She was completely unreasonable.

Chapter 27
Progress

Between 1997, after our parents finalized their divorce, and 2006, when she was approved for Section 8 housing, Siobhan mostly lived with our mother in the small house on Bixby Street.

Both Denise's alcoholism and Sibby's incompletely-diagnosed mental illness progressed. The duo fought constantly. Oftentimes Siobhan would escape to a friend's house for the night. For short intervals she lived with Gwyn and Marco. Once in awhile she'd spend the night with me. She was briefly institutionalized in various mental facilities, and my father even took her back in for short-term stays. But because she had no other long-term choice, she'd always return to our mother's.

When our father moved in with Sibby in the large house on Bend Lane after the divorce, he tried to improve their rapport. He wanted to form a normal bond with his daughter, but failed to recognize that it was impossible to have a healthy relationship with an unhealthy person. Not that he was the picture of perfect health either. His denial was deep.

Nonetheless, he'd gone to therapy with Sibby a few times, even writing her a "promise" letter at the urging of the therapist. He "promised" to watch his temper, exercise patience, and love Siobhan unconditionally. "Promises" he'd break shortly thereafter, throwing his hands up in disgust and alleging that, he'd "tried."

My father and Sibby went on vacation to Salem, Massachusetts in 1998, so Sibby could learn Wiccan history. They spent a weekend together in New York City in 2000, splitting their time between my dad's theatre and the goth underbelly. He even allowed her to paint her bedroom black a few years before kicking her out. As if supporting her morbid interests made him a good father.

But when Sibby was fourteen years old she and Ed had a fight which led to him kicking her out… the first time.

Siobhan moved into Denise's, and a week later they were both arrested for domestic violence, and mandated by the court to attend three therapy sessions together. They fought tooth and nail at each, improving nothing.

Back to their humble abode they went. The fighting continued.

When she was fifteen, Sibby ran away from Denise's. Our mother printed up "missing" fliers with a picture of her youngest adorned in a black cape, which my cousin Mary and I hung around Middletown. We questioned her fellow alternative transients at the indie coffee shop where Siobhan read poetry. No one knew where she was. Three days later she reappeared, unwilling to reveal where she'd been. She felt the secrecy gave her a leg up, and she liked feeling important.

A month later my mother slammed my sister's hand in the door. It was an accident instigated by an avoidable altercation. Actually, all of their disputes could've been circumvented if Denise stopped drinking and Siobhan was correctly medicated. But that would've required change, which neither one of them favored. Repeating the cycle of chaos was much easier.

Voicemails from My Sister

In 2000 Siobhan called me in Boston. It was six-thirty in the morning and I had been fast asleep. She was frantic. "I put our mother in the hospital last night. I split her head open with a chair," she confessed.

"For Christ's sake, Sibby, why?" I was groggy and impatient.

"She tried to kick Chris out so I went buck-wild on her ass," she explained. Chris, her latest boyfriend, was actually pretty normal compared to the bums she typically dated.

"Well, it's her house, Siobhan. If she wants him to leave he should leave."

"No, fuck her drunk ass! I needed to get mine and I'll fuck up anyone who tries to get in the way of my nookie."

I cringed as I pictured my sixteen-year-old sister having sex in the small bedroom we shared as children.

I sighed. It was obvious. Both Denise and Siobhan were progressively declining.

Chapter 28
Sibby's "Moving"

"I'm moving," Siobhan informed me during one of our labored, intermittent phone calls. "To California."

I scoffed. "What else is new?" Siobhan was always "moving," but she never moved.

"No, I'm serious this time. I'm really moving." She was serious every time.

"OK, well good luck to you." I dismissed her claims.

Bipolar schizoaffective people need constant excitement. Since most live a sequestered life, their brains invent delusions.

Siobhan had been "seriously moving" to Maine, Arizona, and across the bridge to Portland since she was eighteen, yet she had only *actually* succeeded in relocating after being evicted from her government-subsidized apartment in 2011 after one too many noise complaints.

Oftentimes her impulsive decision to migrate was inspired by a new friend who offered to become her conservator, without understanding all that that entails.

"His name is Milo and he's a friend of a guy I knew in New York," she explained to me. "He lives in Maine now and he has a spare room that he says I can stay in."

"Jesus Christ, Sibby," I sighed. "Have you even met this guy?"

Voicemails from My Sister

"Technically no, but he's trustworthy, Kate. My friend says he's a really good guy."

Yeah. That proposal never came to fruition.

"Will you help me if I move out there to be closer to you?" She asked, pushing it.

"No. I helped you once and you left town. There's nothing I can do for you. If you want to move, move. But you can't stay here and I can't afford to help you financially."

"No, you wouldn't have to." She began the trip down into the land of ideals in her Alice in Wonderland fantasy. "The program says I can move across state lines. My benefits can be transferred to another state. You wouldn't have to give me a dime."

I knew better. "OK, well, like I said, it's a free country, so if you want to move go ahead."

"I just want to be closer to my sister."

I had been down this road before. Before I knew better. When she first brought up the idea nine years ago in 2005 we talked about where she might find an inexpensive apartment in Hollywood. I entertained fantasies that she might get a part-time job at the restaurant where I was working. We planned to do fun things together, like go to movies at the Hollywood Forever Cemetery and to the Hollywood Bowl. But then her diseased brain would come up with a reason why she couldn't move. Pulling the rug out from under me, just like our mother liked to do. I wouldn't fall for it again.

Voicemails from My Sister

"Look, Sibs, I love you, but you're not going to move. You're having a delusion. We've been through this a million times before."

"I'm not delusional!" She slammed down the phone.

Chapter 29
Investing in Friendship

Our mother died in November 2008. Once Denise's "favorite child," her and Sibby's relationship had devolved into a combative and abusive codependency, which often culminated in a visit from the police.

As her only kin, the house Denise had won in the divorce was passed on to me and Sibby. It was up to us to unload it.

The house was quick to sell, so after our mother's many debts were paid off, the two of us were soon sixteen thousand dollars richer. Because Siobhan had been living off of state assistance for five years at that point, they wanted their money back. After taking their fair share, my sister was left with two thousand dollars.

"You should open a savings account, Sibby," I told her over the phone. I'd been living in California for four years, but was aware of my sister's financial insecurity. Our grandmother had opened a small savings account for her when she was a baby. When she got wind of that at 18, she overdrew from it and ignored the fees. "You should try to iron out your finances now that you have some money."

In true mentally-ill fashion, Siobhan had opened a number of credit cards, then run them up and disregarded the bills. I had seen her bank statement four years earlier and was appalled at the negative balances accumulating in red.

There is no state department assigned to help mentally-ill recipients of social security disability learn how to manage their finances. Bills are sent directly to the conservator (in this case, the state), and paid through their allowance. This is the equivalent of putting a Band-Aid on the problem. There is no attempt to rehabilitate patients with the long-term goal of monetary independence. Their bills are simply paid like magic, without them ever seeing how it was done, or learning how to do it themselves.

A few weeks passed before I spoke to my sister again. "So, did you put your inheritance in the bank?" I inquired.

"No," she replied. "I invested it."

My heart skipped a beat. "What do you mean you *invested* it?" My tone carried a warning. There was no way she'd suddenly learned the stock market and opened a mutual fund.

"I gave it to Chad to invest in his business. I'm a shareholder now."

"You WHAT!?!" I screamed, incredulously. "What business? Who's Chad??"

She began to retreat. "He's a good friend of mine, Kate. He's starting a website and needed investors. I believe in him and I wanted to help."

My head was exploding. "Did you give him everything???"

She paused. Then, "Yes."

"Oh my God, Sibby, are you fucking stupid!? You don't have two pennies to rub together and you gave some guy I've never even heard of all your money!?" I couldn't believe how naive she was… then again, sadly, I kinda could.

"He's trustworthy, Kate. He's a good guy." Her tone was turning defiant.

"How long have you known him?" I challenged.

"Since New Year's." It was February.

"You've known him a month and you gave him two thousand dollars!?!" I was livid. I stopped. I had to detach. "Whelp, there goes all of your inheritance. You'll never see that money again."

Mirroring me, she withdrew as well. "I wouldn't expect you to understand," she dismissed. "Just forget it." She hung up.

Chad promptly disappeared from Siobhan's life, just as quickly as he'd entered it, taking her money and leaving her with nothing. Not even a lesson learned. Her mental illness prevented her from being able to learn from her mistakes. Defiance overtook her, and her brain told her she had been right, despite the outcome. Chad may have stolen her money, but, her brain assured her, that would never happen again.

And, because she kept allowing it, the cycle of broken trust continued.

Chapter 30
Tom

"Punkie, I'm getting married!" Siobhan exclaimed.

She hadn't even been dating anyone a week earlier when I'd talked to her last. "To who, Sibby?" I groaned, afraid of the answer.

"His name is Tom and I met him in the program." Sibby was part of River Valley Services, a state-funded outpatient program for the mentally ill.

I sighed. Another nut-job.

"He's really smart, Punkie. He's in Mensa!" she replied, as if she could read my thoughts.

"OK," I groaned. This was not the first time she'd been "engaged" to someone she'd just met. It was all crazy talk.

"Do you want to meet him? Here, say hi to my sister." I heard her excitedly shove the phone at her fiancée.

"No, Sibby!" I began. I had told her numerous times before to stop trying to make me talk to her friends that I'd never met on the phone. It was so awkward.

"Hi there," Tom greeted cordially.

"Hi. Put Sibby back on the phone," I retorted shortly.

Voicemails from My Sister

That Christmas I went home to Connecticut. Surprisingly, she and Tom were still together, but their relationship had cooled down to just boyfriend/girlfriend status.

"It's good to finally meet you in person," he said, as he reached out to shake my hand. I was impressed. He was tall, attractive, and hygienic, contrary to the majority of Sibby's odious past boyfriends.

We hung out that night, smoking pot and talking. Tom had schizoaffective disorder just like Sibby, but unlike her he was level-headed and calm.

"Do you work?" I asked him.

"Not right now," he answered. "I lost my job in I.T. last year and I haven't been able to get another one."

"Couldn't you just get a job someplace else?" I pressed, echoing my dad's any-job-is-better-than-no-job sentiment.

"I could, but it'd be hard to work at a McDonald's with a 150 IQ."

On Christmas Eve Tom's parents invited us over for coffee and dessert. Kay and Calvin lived in a beautiful colonial-style home in the cozy woods of Haddam. They had been happily married for twenty-five years, and had raised Tom and his sister in this very house.

A quick tour revealed that Tom's family was quaint and modest, their two-level abode warm and inviting. A fire burned in the fireplace, and a Christmas tree stood over a humble pile of gifts. Every room was clean and welcoming, and it seemed like a truly ideal environment in which to grow up.

Voicemails from My Sister

They'd even kept his sister's room exactly as it was, for when she visited from college.

They guided us into their dining room and served me, Tom and Sibby coffee and an array of Christmas-themed treats.

"The den looks nice, Calvin," Sibby complimented. She was at ease, and it was obvious she'd formed a loving relationship with her boyfriend's folks.

"Thank you!" he replied. "We finally finished remodeling," he explained to me.

I smiled. I was so happy for my sister. She seemed... better. Less crazy. Less manic. More stable. *Maybe it's not too late for her to turn her life around,* I hoped.

The three of us hung out every day of my six-day vacation. The more I got to know Tom, the more convinced I was that he was an integral factor in Sibby's positive changes.

For one thing, he complimented her.

"Siobhan has no idea how funny she is," he had said the night before, after she mentioned that bugs listen to her because she can relate to them. She often said crazy things like that. I had learned to dismiss them as the ramblings of a lunatic, but Tom saw them as unique gems from a hilarious mind. Now that he'd mentioned it, I started to appreciate the wacky stuff she said.

Her brain worked tangentially. She'd respond to conversation normally, with a related thought, then, after a beat, say something seemingly unrelated, then conclude with an off-the-wall zinger. Only her bipolar schizoaffective mind could follow the trail, while other participants of the conversation were left thinking, *what?* while collapsing in giggles.

"I used to swim in the quarry," she'd said, in response to Tom's tale about swimming on a hot day. "Walmart is having a sale on bathing suits this week, Punkie," she continued. A beat. "Did you know that O is the oldest letter of the alphabet?"

To "normal" people this thought process was random drivel. To Tom, and now to me, it was gold.

Over the next week Sibby's quirks kept Tom and I in stitches. I noticed hilarious oddities like the fact that she constantly misused phrases.

"I went to Hot Topic yesterday to get some fangs, but they didn't have my size. Anyway, the moral of the story is I've got to call Steve in New York to see if he can send me some for Halloween."

I laughed. "Oh, that's the *moral*, is it?"

Sibby chuckled, then defended herself. "Yeah, the lesson is I can't rely on Hot Topic."

She wasn't wrong.

I remembered the way she used to wake me up when we were little. She'd lie perfectly still with her face to mine. Nose to nose, I'd open my eyes to see her wide eyes bulging like a cracked-out clown.

"Jesus Christ!" I'd scream. What a way to be awoken.

Voicemails from My Sister

She'd learned from our father that scaring people is funny. She'd hide in the stairwell at Gumma's and run out screaming, "Raaaahhhh!" when I'd exit the bathroom.

"Ahhh! Goddammit, Sibby!" She got me every time.

Sibby wasn't above a dad joke either.

"I'm hungry," I'd say.

"Nice to meet you, I'm Siobhan." Fully committed to the joke, she'd stick out her hand to shake mine.

I'd roll my eyes. Then smile.

My sister was an adorable comedic genius.

Chapter 31
Hoarding

Every time I'd go home to Connecticut I'd assign myself the task of cleaning my sister's apartment. A gross hoarder, she lived in filth because she'd simply never developed the skills to clean.

"I spent all day cleaning my apartment!" she'd excitedly brag to me.

But when I'd get there, I'd walk into the same disgusting mess as always. She truly didn't know what clean was.

In 2009, cautiously, I entered the dwelling I hadn't set foot in for a year, dreading the wreckage that had manifested.

Siobhan lived in a cramped one-room cubicle, her stove six inches from her bed. She had stuffed my mother's huge, old wooden bed frame, as well as a couch and desk into this tiny compartment, and every surface was piled with clothes and peppered with garbage: food wrappers, cigarette butts, crumpled up napkins. The sink was full of dishes that had been there for months from the looks of the caked-on food and the swarms of fruit flies. It reeked of cigarettes, and the one and only window was sealed shut, shades drawn. *God, she's just like my mother,* I thought.

Trepidatiously, I entered the bathroom. Twenty-odd half empty bottles of Suave shampoo and conditioner cluttered her grimy shower. Dirt lined the tub, and piles of hair sat in clumps, as if she couldn't be bothered to travel to the garbage can to throw them out after dislodging them from the drain. The floor around the toilet was wet, and a 12-pack

Voicemails from My Sister

of toilet paper was soaked up to the top roll. "Sibby, what the hell happened in here?" I scolded.

"Oh yeah, the toilet overflowed," she dismissed. *Oh my God.*

"Go to Walmart with Tom while I start cleaning out some of this stuff," I instructed.

"No, you'll throw my stuff away," she argued.

"Sibby, I promise not to throw anything away," I lied. "It's just too crowded in here and I need cleaning supplies."

As soon as they left I broke my promise and started hauling things out to the dumpster, beginning with the piles of phone books she'd collected. I filled trash bags with garbage and made piles of clothes to take to my dad's to wash. By the time Tom and Sibby returned you could almost see the floor. I instructed them to go right back to Walmart for more supplies so I could continue binge-cleaning in peace.

"Wait a minute, where are my phone books?" Sibby demanded.

"I threw them out, Sibby. You don't need them. You can look up phone numbers on the internet now."

"You threw them away? Goddammit, Kate, those were irreplaceable!"

Tom and I looked at each other and started to laugh. Siobhan, aware that our laughter was a compliment, not a judgement, melted into hysterics as well, subconsciously patting herself on the back for having made a funny. Her anger at my misdoing vanished, as she felt a part of. That feeling of acceptance penetrated her disease and she recognized the truth: her phonebooks were *not* irreplaceable, and she was loved.

The following morning I picked her up. She and Tom were sleeping when I knocked on the door and opened it thinking they'd be ready to go. "Oh, sorry," I began, then noted how my efforts at decluttering had been partially undone in the twelve hours I'd been away. A piece of pizza with a bite taken out of it sat atop her headboard on a bed of cigarette ash.

"You were supposed to be ready to go," I scolded her.

"Quit bitching at me!" she shouted. She was *not* a morning person.

Stumbling out of bed, she picked a pair of jeans off the sticky floor and began putting them on, then picked up the piece of pizza and took a bite.

"Siobhan, no!" I tried to stop her, a split second too late. "Gross! Don't eat that! It was in a pile of cigarette ashes!"

"Bitch and moan, bitch and moan," she chastised, as she continued to eat the dirty pie.

"You're disgusting," I replied.

The next morning she met me at our grandmother's house. This time, it was me who was the late riser.

I'd been up late the night before going through old files, and had been munching on a cut-up bell pepper, which I'd left on a plate on the dining room table.

Siobhan let herself in, and I descended the stairs to greet her.

Voicemails from My Sister

"Where's my bell pepper?" I accused, when I saw the plate was gone.

"I threw it away," she said, as if I should be grateful, "so you wouldn't get food poisoning." Oh, the logic of a crazy person.

I stopped visiting Connecticut after cutting off communication with my dad in 2011, so she no longer reaped the benefits (although she never did recognize them as such) of having someone detail her home once a year.

In 2018 she ran into an old family friend.

Martin had been friends with me, my mother, and Sibby since 1996. He was an old stoner who worked as a cook at the hospital and picked up part-time gigs bartending at the Eagle's Club or short-order line-cooking at O'Malley's. He bumped into Siobhan at the grocery store and invited her over for Thanksgiving, as she mentioned she had nowhere to go.

A week later he called me, drunk. "Hi Kate, I just wanted to let you know what's going on with Sibby," he slurred. "I went over there to pick her up and I saw in her apartment and, Kate, it was a disaster," he continued. "So I told her I'd help her out. I went over there to clean today. I was there all day and I basically only got the kitchen area cleaned. Oh my God, Katie, it's like a hoarder's house!"

"I know, Martin. I know," I exhaled.

"No, Kate, I mean, it's *really* bad. She had no clean dishes. There were ants everywhere. Some of the food in her fridge was moldy."

Voicemails from My Sister

I stopped him. "Wait a minute — she has food?"

I had been sending my sister take-out twice a week, as she claimed her EBT card didn't afford her enough for groceries since state funding had been cut.

"Oh yeah, she's got a fridge full of food, but not one clean dish to put it on," he replied.

Did she honestly not think she had food? Was she just too lazy to wash a dish and make herself something? No. The truth was she lacked the life skill of washing the correct dishes and preparing a meal in them. She had never been taught how to care for herself.

She got a pet hamster in 2011. "His name is Blue," she told me over the phone.

"Because that's what color he's going to be when you kill him?" I deadpanned

As expected, less than a month later she couldn't find it.

"Jesus Christ, Sibby. What do you mean you can't find it?" I was so sad for this poor animal whose short life of inhaling second-hand smoke was now likely concluding by being squished under a waterbed.

"Gimme a break, Kate," she sassed. "Everybody loses a hamster at least once in their life."

Chapter 32
Squatters

Siobhan was never taught boundaries. As a result, she became instantly attached to people. Watch out, or you might become her best friend or fiancée within a day of meeting her.

When Sibby was approved for Section 8 housing she began allowing people to crash at her place.

"Who's there?" I'd ask, hearing a voice in the background while we were on the phone.

"Oh, my new friend Jake. He's staying here for awhile because he lost his job and his apartment."

"Sibby, you can't just let people live with you." I tried to protect my naive sister.

"He has nowhere to go, Kate!" she defended him vehemently, as if he were her son.

"Jesus Christ, Sibby. You're not running a flophouse!"

But Siobhan was lonely. Being alone meant being alone with her thoughts, and that scared her.

Soon Sibby and Jake had a fight and he moved out. No sooner had he slammed the door behind him than another down-on-their-luck "friend" of Sibby's had taken his place.

"Genevive, my new best friend, is living with me now. Do you want to say hi?"

Voicemails from My Sister

"Dammit Sibby, no! What do you mean she's living with you?"

"She left her baby daddy and needed a place to live so I offered her my couch. I figured why not help out a friend, you know? I would want someone to do the same for me if I were in that position."

Sibby was in an elevated state of mania. I couldn't get a word in.

"Besides, she's gonna help me out. She's gonna take over as my conservator and help me get my finances in order. Then, when she's able, she's gonna pay me rent. I'm gonna have a roommate, Kate."

Sounds nice, doesn't it? But it wouldn't quite go down that way.

A few weeks later Genevive disappeared with Sibby's laptop, iPod, and cell phone.

"Well Sibby, you can't just automatically trust everyone the second you meet them." I tried to instill the lesson in her.

"I know," she claimed. But within weeks she gave a new acquaintance a key to her apartment, allowing them to come and go as they pleased.

"Alright, but don't call me crying when this person steals from you too," I warned.

"No Punkie, this time it's different."

Voicemails from My Sister

Of course it was. It was always different in Sibby's crazy brain. In reality, she'd repeat the same mistakes over and over again, expecting different results.

In 2013 Sibby called me in a panic. "Kate, I have Lyme disease."

Her frenzy no longer fazed me.

"So get it treated," I responded impatiently.

"I would, but I don't have a ride to the doctor."

Somehow her problems always became someone else's.

"Sibby has Lyme disease," I confided in my boyfriend that night.

Without missing a beat, and 75% serious, he exclaimed, "Jesus Christ, does she have a deer living with her now!?"

Honestly, I wouldn't have been surprised.

Chapter 33
You Can't Have Nice Things

Bipolar schizoaffective disorder is manipulative. It transforms good things into bad in the mind.

In 2011 I started sending my sister take-out a few times a week. One day she called me during a bipolar schizoaffective episode and claimed that I'd told her not to ask me to send her food anymore until she had paid me back for all of the food I'd already sent her. This accusation enraged me.

"I never said anything like that," I spat.

"Yes, you did," she argued.

Fuck this fucking disease. How dare it turn my good deeds into something negative. Shame on it for convincing my sister that I was a reneger.

I knew how to get even. "No, Sibby. You're having a delusion."

"I'M NOT DELUSIONAL!"

I smiled.

Fighting the victim of the brain disorder was the only way I knew to get revenge on the sickness, since I couldn't extract the malady from my sister's head and fight it on its own.

Fuck this mind disease that warped the truth.

Voicemails from My Sister

Why couldn't it just leave Sibby alone and let her have something nice? I had loved sending her food. It made me feel good, and it gave her something to look forward to. Now I couldn't do it anymore because the act had been poisoned in her brain. It was no longer an admirable action. It was tainted.

Bipolar schizoaffective disorder wants its victims to remain unhappy. It paints good people as bad in the brain so the victim/patient will distrust everyone and isolate themselves.

It is like alcoholism in that way. Addiction is sometimes explained in 12-Step programs as "a disease that wants you dead, but will settle for making you miserable." I would define my sister's diagnosis the same way. Bipolar schizoaffective disorder, like alcoholism/addiction, twists favorable things into unfavorable in the mind. A delusion from bipolar schizoaffective disorder propels the patient into a state of psychosis, thus their only relief comes from mood-altering pharmaceuticals. Likewise, the truth-bending of the alcoholic mind pushes the addict towards a drink or drug for relief.

And, like addiction, it only gets worse.

Chapter 34
Scattered

Sibby was too irresponsible to be trusted with material things. Once I gave her $20, which she promptly lost. I stopped giving her money after that, opting instead to buy her food or clothing directly.

My father bought her multiple laptops and iPods for Christmas, which would magically disappear. More often than not it was her good-for-nothing compatriots stealing from her. But sometimes she simply lost stuff under piles of garbage in her house.

I called her one day in March 2005. "Hey, can you email me the pictures Dad sent you that he scanned out of the photo album?"

"I can't," she replied, nonplussed, then audibly took a drag off a cigarette. "My laptop got stolen."

Our father had just given her a new laptop for Christmas.

"What do you mean!?" I exclaimed. I couldn't believe she'd lost *another* computer.

"I loaned it to Pete so he could put some music on it for me for DJing and he left it in his car overnight and his car got broken into and someone stole it." Her anxiety rose as she relived the catastrophe.

"That sounds awfully suspicious, Sibby. Are you sure he didn't just steal it and make up that story?"

Voicemails from My Sister

"No, Kate." She automatically defended him, without even considering my theory. "He's honest… or it might be on my coffee table."

I paused. An incredulous beat. Then — "What!? You *just* said it was stolen out of Pete's car!"

"It was. I think," I heard her try halfheartedly to organize her memory. "Or maybe he brought it back and it's here somewhere."

How could someone be so scattered?

"Well, you better find it because if Dad finds out you lost that laptop he'll never get you another one."

To my knowledge she never found it. But to be fair it could still be on her desk.

I wonder if, subconsciously, Sibby lost her expensive belongings because she knew she couldn't handle the responsibility of owning valuable things. Perhaps her brain was protecting her from accountability by immediately shirking it.

If it's lost then I don't have to look after it anymore, her anxiety may have subliminally directed. *After all, guarding this laptop makes me feel nervous, and that's not healthy.* Perhaps misplacing things was actually a form of self-care.

"Don't lose it," my father warned right after Sibby unwrapped the brand-new electronic device. That was a threat. *If you do, I'll rage at you,* was the subtext… Maybe her mind was leading a rebellion against my overbearing father.

"I won't," she robotically replied.

Voicemails from My Sister

We'll show him, I imagined her disobedient brain comfort. *We'll lose it and make a fool out of him yet again!*

Whatever the reason, Sibby could not hold onto valuable items.

Chapter 35
Conspiracy Theories

In 2006 my car was vandalized in Los Angeles.

"Oh shit…" Sibby said, when I told her over the phone, in a tone that suggested she knew something she didn't want to tell me.

"What?" I snapped, annoyed.

"I know who did it," she revealed.

"Siobhan, you don't know who broke my car windshield. I'm 3,000 miles away!" I retorted.

"No, I do. It was Derek." Her ex-boyfriend, who lived in Connecticut.

"Sibby, Derek did not travel across the country to damage my vehicle," I tried to reason with the kook.

Her touched brain scrambled to cobble together logic. "He has connections, Kate," she whispered. "He's a Mason."

Oh, for Christ's sake. Here we go.

It was normal for my sister's brain to manipulate an outside incident into a personal attack. Paranoid delusions are a symptom of schizoaffective disorder.

Sibby and I would speak on the phone a few times a week.

"I'm at Pete's pool," she said one June afternoon.

Voicemails from My Sister

"Pete has a pool?" I replied.

"SHHHHH!" she commanded. "Be quiet! Someone could hear you!"

"I'm alone in my apartment, you nut!" I shouted back, before slamming down the phone. I simply could not and *would* not humor her disease.

As if it changed with the waxing and waning of the tides, Sibby's crazy would subside for a few weeks. Then it would return, as if coinciding with the phases of the moon.

"Punkie," Siobhan whispered into the receiver one evening. "People are looking for me. I was set up, and now people are searching for me to kill me."

I let out a long sigh. *Should I just hang up?* I did not.

"Why, Sibby? For what?"

"I can't tell you because the government is listening in. They tapped my phone."

Christ almighty.

"Sibby, that's crazy. No one is listening in on this phone call and no one is looking for you to kill you. You're not that important."

"You don't know, Kate!" She started to hyperventilate. "You don't know what I got involved in! I did some bad shit. Some really bad shit, Kate, and now they're gonna kill me!" she sobbed.

Voicemails from My Sister

None of this was true. How do I know? Because nothing ever came of it. Two weeks later she forgot all about this crazy allegation, and we had a nice talk about our plans for her upcoming visit.

Then the roller coaster dropped again. "I can't leave my house, Punkie," Sibby sobbed down the phone. "There's a tracking device in me."

Good God.

"No, there isn't," I calmly replied.

"There is, Kate! I went to the emergency room to have a routine procedure — something I can't tell you about," (of course not), "and they gave me an injection with a chip in it to track my whereabouts."

"Who are 'they,' Sibby?"

"The gestapo."

Lord in heaven.

"Fine, then I guess you have to stay home," I humored myself.

"Yeah, but I have to stay very still because they also installed cameras in my apartment."

Chapter 36
Sibby the Celebrity

"I wrote a song for a famous singer, but I never told you about it," Sibby disclosed to me in 2004.

'This oughta be good.'

"Who? Which famous singer hired you to write them a song?" I challenged.

"Britney Spears."

I snorted. "What song do you think you wrote for Britney Spears?" My anger increased. "And how, pray tell, did you get this song to her?"

"'I'm a Slave 4 U.' Pete's dad has a connection. I gave it to him and he gave it to her."

I could not believe this bullshit.

"Then why aren't you rich, Sibby?"

"I refused payment because I didn't want the fame," she calmly justified.

I laughed out loud. "That's a new one. How humble of you."

She remained calm and continued, "That's right. She wanted to pay me but I said no, Britney, I want you to have this. I'm not doing it for the money. I want to give it to you because you deserve it."

Voicemails from My Sister

The next day I called her case worker. "She lies all the time," I told her.

"She's not lying," she explained. "She believes these things are true."

I'd never heard of such a thing.

"That's what delusions are. Siobhan's brain constructs memories of things that didn't happen, and she believes them," she continued.

Three years after her schizoaffective diagnosis I was finally learning what it was. My sister wasn't full of shit, she was severely mentally ill.

Chapter 37
Sibby's L.A. Visit

In July 2010, when I was thirty-one and Sibby twenty-six, she flew out to Los Angeles to visit me for eleven days.

Over the past seven years of living three-thousand miles apart, our relationship had had its ups and downs. We'd talk on the phone a few times a week. Depending entirely on Sibby's state of mind, these conversations ranged from amicable to abusive, oftentimes within the course of a five-minute call. Sometimes she was in a good mood when she'd ring. Sharing Shifty Shell-Shock's next concert date in case I wanted to attend, for example, Sibby attempted to connect with me. Her disposition positive at first, the atmosphere shifted as I mentioned, yet again, that I was not a fan of Shifty. "You can go for me," she argued.

"That makes no sense, Sibby," I retorted.

"Fine, fuck you then!" she bellowed, before slamming down the phone.

Other times, she called in a state of hysteria. "Punkie, I might be dying!" she once declared, trying to rile me up. She hated being panicked alone.

Seeking balance, I calmly replied, "What is it this time?"

"I stepped on a rusty nail outside my apartment and mom and dad never got me a tetanus shot," she hastily explained. "Derek said I could get blood poisoning from the bacteria if I've never been vaccinated." She confused the facts.

Voicemails from My Sister

"So go to the doctor, Sibby," I rationalized.

"I would, but I don't have a ride," she explained.

"Well, I guess you're gonna die then," I concluded.

She delivered her dying speech. "OK, well, I love you and I just wanted to tell you that even though we've had our rough times, you're still my sister and I love you."

"OK, Godspeed," I concluded, and hung up on her.

Despite these colorful interactions, I thought a trip to Hollywood was a good idea. It was an impulsive decision inspired by a congenial ten-minute chat. I wanted to do something nice for my sister, who rarely left her apartment, so I offered to pay for her plane ticket and she gratefully accepted.

On July 10 at eleven p.m. my boyfriend Austin and I picked her up from LAX.

Her odor reached the car before she did. "Sibby, you reek of cigarettes!" I exclaimed, beginning the trip with an insult. Her face fell and she glanced to Austin, embarrassingly trying to ascertain if he agreed. Non-judgmentally, he gave her a hug. "It's good to see you, Sibs," he said.

"It's good to see you too," she replied.

She got in the car and we began the forty-minute drive home. I lowered the windows as the scent of body odor peppered the air. *Uh,* I thought. *Those poor other passengers.* I felt so bad for whoever got stuck sitting near her.

"Take a shower, please," I instructed as soon as we entered our apartment. She took off her dirty sneakers, which she'd been wearing with no socks, and a waft of sour fumes hit me in the face. "Oh my God, Sibby!" I automatically exclaimed. "I'm throwing those shoes away! They reek! I'll buy you new ones tomorrow," I promised. She didn't argue.

After her shower she opened her suitcase and another wave of smells filled the apartment. "Did you empty an ashtray in here?" I asked seriously. The contents of her case stank of stale tobacco.

I gave her some of my clothes to wear and hauled her luggage to the laundry room, emptying its contents into the washer. But the wash and dry barely extinguished the odor. Her clothes were permanently cigarette-scented.

When I came back up from the laundry room, Siobhan and Austin were sitting on the couch talking.

"Kate said I can't masturbate while I'm here," she overshared, "which is hard 'cause I masturbate every day. Well actually, I don't masturbate every day, but when I do, I can be there for days. I mean, if someone didn't call me…"

I was both embarrassed and amused.

"I think I'm gonna change the water in this." I picked up the bong.

"Yeah, that bong water doesn't look too healthy," Sibby agreed. "You're a good mom. And that was hard for me to say."

Good lord. This might be a very long trip.

Chapter 38
Shifty, Where Are You?

Siobhan was obsessed with the singer Shifty from Crazy Town, and no, the irony of his band's name was not lost on me. He was to perform at the Roxy on the third night of her trip, and at Les Deux on the fifth. I agreed to take her to both clubs so she could see her idol.

I loaned Siobhan a sexy outfit to wear to the hotspot: a black miniskirt and off-the-shoulder mesh top, which she paired with her own fishnets and Doc Marten boots. I straightened her long, thick hair and vowed to take her for a haircut while she was in town, as it was obvious she hadn't visited a salon in years. She put on some of my bangle bracelets and lamented not being able to wear my hoop earrings, as she'd let her pierced ears close up after multiple infections. Her pasty skin wouldn't hold her cheap makeup, so I gave her a tube of my red lipstick and told her we could do face masks the following night.

We looked hot as we stood in the crowd for the Roxy. "We're here to see Shifty," Siobhan randomly told another person in line. Ever since she was a child she'd arbitrarily talk to strangers.

"I don't think he's here tonight," she replied.

Oh no, I thought. *Sibby was so looking forward to this.* We asked other people around us.

"No, Zion's performing," they confirmed.

Voicemails from My Sister

To make absolutely sure, we approached the woman in the ticket booth. "Shifty cancelled," she verified.

"Oh Sibby, I'm so sorry!" I mourned. "We'll see him Thursday. Do you wanna get a drink at the Rainbow?" I offered. "I mean, we look too hot to just go home." We made our way next door to the Rainbow Room. Seated at a table on the patio she ordered a whiskey sour and I ordered a glass of Pinot Grigio. We asked a man who was making eyes at us to take a few pictures as proof of our fun night out together.

Three nights later we repeated our primping and drove to Les Deux, another Hollywood venue. "We're finally gonna see Shifty!" I tried to boost my sister's enthusiasm. It was the fifth day of our visit, and we were both coming to the realization that eleven days was much too long a trip. Nonetheless, I was shelling out forty bucks for us to get into this douchey club, so I was determined that my sister have a good time.

Les Deux was packed and the music was blaring. Holding her hand, I led Sibby through the crowd towards one of the bars in a quieter room. "We're here to see Shifty," I revealed to the bartender, mirroring her outgoing spirit from a few nights earlier. I looked at Sibby and could tell that she was triggered. The volume of the music and the noise of the club-goers overwhelmed her and she retreated into her own head.

"He's not here tonight," the bartender replied.

"Oh, no!" Sibby whined.

"What?" I echoed.

"He cancelled at the last minute," the drink-slinger confirmed. Now I was pissed.

Voicemails from My Sister

"Let's just go," Sibby said.

"No! I just spent a lot of money to get us in here," I whined. "Let's at least hang out for a little bit." I ordered her a whiskey sour and a vodka tonic for myself. I made my way over to a couch and sat down, observing the purple walls and old-fashioned furniture that made this space look kinda like a hipster speakeasy. Sibby walked in the opposite direction and stood by herself in the corner. I was annoyed. She did not want to be here.

I drank my drink quickly then approached her. "Let's walk around and see the rest of the rooms," I offered, still trying to boost her mood. We made our way outside to the back patio. Fire-dancers adorned in loin cloths and headpieces spun poles with both ends aflame. "Sibby, look!" I pointed them out to her. Surely she'd think that was cool. She tried to smile, but she was too deep down the rabbit hole of depression and isolation for me to pull her out.

"We can go if you want," I relented.

"Thank you," she replied. She had barely taken a sip of her cocktail. She placed it on a table and I picked it up and slugged it while we exited, so as not to waste it.

"Sibby, I'm so sorry you didn't get to see Shifty while you were here," I lamented. "What the fuck is wrong with him, cancelling twice?"

"Maybe he was sick," she defended.

Three years later I was working at Abramowitz Deli in West Hollywood when Shifty came in and sat at one of my tables. He was with two beautiful girls, and was obviously heavily intoxicated. After entering their order into the computer I returned with their Dr. Brown's sodas. "My sister is your biggest fan," I revealed. He looked up at me with foggy eyes, and one of the girls put her arm around him, as if to say, 'See, you *are* still relevant.' "We went to see you perform twice when she was out here visiting me, but you never showed up." Unsure of what to say, he just looked at me. Then I got an idea. "Would you talk to her if I called her right now?" I brazenly requested.

"Sure," he replied, perhaps because that was the only word his drunk mouth could spit.

I ran to get my cell phone, and called Siobhan. Thankfully, she answered. "Siobhan," I singsonged, "guess who wants to say hi to you?"

"Who?" I heard her reply, as I handed the phone to Mr. Shell-Shock.

"Hello?" he muttered, clearly having forgotten who he was talking to and why. "This is Seth."

Good Christ, I thought. "It's Shifty," I chimed in, expecting to propel my sister to excitement.

"Oh hey, what's up," Sibby replied nonchalantly.

"Nothing, what are you doing?" the rock star continued flatly.

"Just chillin'," I heard Sibby reply.

What the fuck was this casual attitude? I thought, annoyed. *This was supposed to make her life. Why was she talking to her idol like he was just another one of her boring friends?* I

Voicemails from My Sister

took the phone from him. "Sibby, it's Shifty," I pushed. "Aren't you excited?"

"I am Punkie," she dully responded. "Thank you so much for this."

Chapter 39
Raging Waters

On the fourth day of her trip Sibby and I went to Raging Waters Water Park with my co-worker, Brian, and his brother, Mark. We smoked pot on the drive.

It was a sweltering day and we were all anxious to cool off in the water. Our first stop was the wave pool, to get wet before standing in the long lines for waterslides. After a quick soak we made our way to Neptune's Fury. The line for this popular ride was so long that it ended at the ground level of a winding staircase. The wooden scaffolding leading to the top of the slide consisted of quadratic sections of stairs, separated by platforms. Railings and fences protected park-goers from falling, but the sway of the damp wood made rickety noises, which caused Siobhan anxiety.

"Oh shit!" Sibby exclaimed, grabbing the rail as the structure shook from another person zooming down the slide.

We all laughed at her reaction, then switched back to gossiping as the line moved upward. Brian and Mark were getting along well with my sister, which put me at ease. I had been afraid she'd feel outnumbered, as she often did when I had a friend present, but she did not.

"I DJ on Waste Heap Radio sometimes," she shared with her new friends. Waste Heap was a public access radio show produced by her hoodlum vampire buddy, Mike. Every now and again Mike would remember he ran this venture and allow DJ Sibby Yup Yup a four-hour slot to play her favorite songs. I'd listen when she was on air, enjoying the juxtaposition of her playlist. "Two Buffalos" followed Marilyn Manson,

Voicemails from My Sister

early Madonna preceded "Rubber Ducky," and "I'm An Asshole" was interrupted by Gem and the Holograms.

"Yo, that's cool," Mark, a budding rap artist, encouraged. "I'll give you one of my CDs. Maybe you can play it on your show sometime."

We climbed another set of stairs as the line moved quickly. Brian hopped on the banister.

"BE CAREFUL!" Sibby screamed.

Confused, Brian slid off the rail, as people turned to see what had caused the outburst.

"Sibby, relax," I gaslit. She was starting to embarrass me in front of my friends.

The row of people moved forward, and we ascended to the next landing.

"Damn, it's nice up here," Mark commented, leaning on the handrail to take in the view.

Sibby began to hyperventilate. She grabbed both balusters, steadying herself in the center, and looked down at the stairs.

"Sibby, stop it. Come on." I tried to pry her hands loose as the line continued to move.

"KATE, NO! STOP IT! LEAVE ME ALONE! DON'T TOUCH ME!" She started to cry as a panic attack overtook her.

The crowd craned their necks as Sibby inhaled and exhaled quickly, frozen like a statue, grasping the rails.

Voicemails from My Sister

"Yo, it's OK," Brian soothed.

"It's all good, Sibs," Mark echoed.

Their words calmed her a little, but she still could not let go or move.

A ride attendant descended the stairs. Word had made its way to the top that a girl was freaking the fuck out at the halfway point. "Honey, would you like to come sit at the top with me?" he soothed.

She still could not look up. "… Yes," she spat. She reminded me of my mother, who had had a nervous disorder, the results of which caused occasional public embarrassment.

"OK, take my hand. I'll guide you." It was obvious he'd dealt with customers' fear of heights before.

Hesitantly Sibby released her death grip with her left hand and grabbed his right.

"Good!" he praised, patiently waiting for her to make the move up the next step.

"I can't move," she cried. She was frozen in fear.

"You got this," a girl behind us encouraged. "Yeah," other strangers chimed in. "You can do it." My heart broke at the outpouring of kindness, and my eyes dampened.

Allowing these reassuring words to motivate her, Sibby began to climb slowly.

Voicemails from My Sister

"Great job!" the park employee congratulated, as her pace increased and her fear diminished.

She grasped the waterpark worker's hands with both of hers, and they scaled the rest of the scaffolding and reached the top.

Applause broke out among the patrons, strengthening my faith in humanity and comforting my sister. Sometimes people could be very kind. That always took me by surprise.

When Brian, Mark, and I reached the apex, Sibby was sitting on the ground, drinking a soda and laughing with the attendants.

"You doing better?" I singsonged.

"Yes." She smiled.

Her new friend the park employee set us up on our raft: me in front, Sibby behind. "Ready?" he motivated.

"Yeah!" she exclaimed. Sibby's fear had turned to excitement. She was now one hundred percent in the fun zone.

"One, two, three!" He pushed us down the slide. Our raft raced down the enclosed, plastic tube.

We began to laugh as our adrenaline spiked and we were overtaken by thrill.

My sister cackled in my ear as our boat sloshed up the sides of the chute as we sharply cut a corner.

The echo of the next rider's yells exacerbated our joy. Sibby understood the excitement that came with the beginning of a ride, having just experienced it herself, and she chuckled in anticipation for them. When Sibby felt a part of things, her anxiety decreased and her happiness increased. I could understand that. It sucks to feel alone.

The tube spat us out into the pool at the bottom, where we submerged for a second before floating to the surface. We grabbed onto our tube, which we'd fallen off, and walked it to the small pool's stairs.

Grinning from ear to ear, Sibby chortled, "Can we do that again?"

Chapter 40
Spiritual Solution

The next day Austin and I took Sibby to Marina Del Rey to meet his sister and her family. Tanya, her husband Greg, and their two children, Stacy and Candice, were the picture of perfect health. Raw foodists, they lived in an open, feng shui-ed condo on the beach. Tanya and Greg home-schooled the eight-and twelve-year olds, and the family meditated together as part of their daily practice. Meeting these hippies was gonna be great for Sibby.

"I talk to cats," Siobhan revealed to my boyfriend's family, as she approached the pet's kitty tower. She stroked Potato's fur, then put her face to his face. "You have mystical powers," she whispered, then paused. "He says he knows," she disclosed to the six of us, who stood watching uncomfortably.

They took us for a walk on the beach. Sensing this family's positive energy, Siobhan began to open up about her spirituality. "I'm not strictly satanic anymore," she admitted. I hadn't known that. The last I'd heard was when I suggested she go to trade school to learn an employable skill, and she'd replied with, "Kate, they don't have trade schools for demonology." I dropped the subject and never brought it up again. *Well, it's good to see she's progressing,* I thought.

"What do you want to do for a job?" Tanya inquired, after it came out that my sister had been unemployed for years.

"I thought about that, and I started to make a list," Sibby replied. "Actress, model, dancer, singer…" she began.

Voicemails from My Sister

Tanya's eyes met mine and I shook my head. *Don't even bother,* I tried to telecommunicate, but Tanya pushed on.

"Well, how about a temporary job somewhere in your neighborhood while you work on achieving those goals?" She spoke to Sibby as if she were level-headed, not realizing my sister's disease prevented her from being able to differentiate between small and large ambitions.

Two days later Sibby and I ventured on a drive to Santa Monica, but I took a wrong turn and we ended up pointed towards Marina Del Rey. I called Tanya from the car. "We're on our way towards you. Might you be up for a visit?" Of course they were, she welcomed. We drove back to their apartment.

Siobhan liked them. I was glad. I'd spent so much energy wishing she'd extricate herself from her negative friends; it was hopeful to see her gravitating towards these positive souls on her own. They embraced us as we entered.

"We just juiced a coconut," Tanya announced, pouring us each a glass. Siobhan, who normally couldn't stand the taste of anything natural, hummed, "mmmmm," as she swallowed.

The family had been studying religion when we arrived. "I was raised Jewish," Tanya explained, "but I want my kids to explore all of the different religions."

"Our parents did the opposite," I said. "They didn't teach us any religion, and said we could learn when we were older if we were interested." I scanned the pile of religious textbooks spread out on the floor: *Introduction to Hinduism, Christianity 101,* and *Buddhism for Beginners.*

"Mom was a Buddhist," Sibby said. I scoffed.

"No she wasn't, Sibby." Our mom was nothing but an angry drunk.

"It's cool that you guys pray together," she complimented.

"You can join us if you want," Greg offered. "We'll do a Buddhist prayer, in honor of your mom," he continued. We all joined hands and closed our eyes while Greg read, "May I be free from fear. May I be free from suffering. May I be happy. May I be filled with loving kindness. May you be free from fear. May you be free from suffering. May you be happy. May you be filled with loving kindness. May all people everywhere be happy and filled with loving kindness." When I opened my eyes I saw that Siobhan's were filled with tears.

"That was beautiful," she lamented.

"Thank you so much for inviting us over," I said when they hugged us goodbye. "We were on our way to the beach, but we took a wrong turn," I continued.

"You didn't take a wrong turn," Greg corrected, and I understood what he meant. "You took the right turn." Sibby and I smiled, as we both agreed.

Chapter 41
Sibby Makes the Blotter

Over the years Siobhan became well acquainted with the Middletown police department. They had been summoned numerous times to intervene in domestic violence disputes between her and our mother. Denise and Sibby had been arrested a few times for disturbing the peace.

In the spring of 2015 Siobhan was arrested for physical violence twice in the span of two months. The first time she attempted to run over her ex-boyfriend with her car:

> *May 26, 2015 - Police arrested a 30-year-old Middletown woman who is accused of trying to run down her ex-boyfriend and nearly hitting people gathered at a Memorial Day yard sale.*
> *Police responded to Farm Hill Road just after 2 p.m. on Monday and met with the victim who said his ex-girlfriend, Siobhan Russell, 30, had gone over the center line of the street and tried to run him off the road, police said.*
> *The victim told police he had to brake and swerve hard to avoid the crash, which happened close to a yard sale where several people were gathered. He added that Russell screamed obscenities at him, said she was going to "get" him and that she was going to kill everyone at the yard sale, then sped off, police said.*
> *Just a few minutes before the incident, the victim had received a call from his mother, who said Russell had assaulted her and damaged her property.*

> *Russell was taken into custody, held in lieu of $50,000 bond and charged with third-degree criminal mischief, attempt to commit third-degree criminal mischief, two counts of second-degree breach of peace, second-degree threatening, reckless driving and failure to drive right.*
> *She is due in court on Tuesday.*

Seven weeks later she stabbed her friend:

> *July 15, 2015 - A heated argument between friends ended when a city woman stabbed a man who refused to leave her apartment, according to police.*
> *On the evening of July 15, authorities were called to Hollow Park for a stabbing, and found Vince Scapelli, 30, sitting on the curb with a puncture wound on his back, according to a report.*
> *There was blood down his pants, Middletown police say, although it's unclear from the report how Scapelli had gotten to the park.*
> *Scapelli later said in a sworn statement that he and a friend, Siobhan Russell, 31, went to her apartment, argued, then the dispute turned physical when he refused to leave.*
> *Russell "picked up a knife and began lunging at him, holding the handle," the arrest report says, so he grabbed her hand to block the knife swipes with one hand and with the other held her hip to prevent the attack.*
> *"Despite his efforts," police indicate, "one of her lunges made it over his left shoulder and the knife entered his back."*

> Russell allegedly admitted to asking him to leave and initially denied stabbing Scapelli, saying she "may have had a pen to defend herself."
> Upon further interview, authorities say, Russell allowed that she did grab a knife but only to defend herself and may have stabbed her friend, but "was unsure."
> Scapelli was charged with disorderly conduct and is due to appear in court July 30, while Russell was arrested for third-degree assault and is due in court on July 24.

Perhaps she has seasonal psychosis. In April 2011 she called to tell me that she "could not come to visit" for reasons that she "could not tell me."

We had spent the prior week planning her second visit to Los Angeles. We'd gone over dates, and decided that a six-day visit was ideal this time, as her previous eleven-day stint had proven too long for both our sanities. I'd purchased her round-trip plane ticket and we'd gone over the details of who was to drive her to and from Bradley airport. I'd taken care to get a non-stop flight, as the stress of having to switch planes overwhelmed her. We'd even gone over her packing list, as the first time she'd nonsensically brought nine bottles of Suave shampoo so we could wash our hair. I was looking forward to this second visit. Of course her disease had to creep up and ruin it.

"Oh yeah, she usually goes crazy around this time of year," her nurse informed me. I had called her to let her know that Sibby would *not* be needing a week-long supply of Abilify, after all. "Better to plan a trip in winter," she continued.

Voicemails from My Sister

The RN offered to write a letter explaining Sibby's mental illness to the airline so that I could obtain a refund for her non-refundable ticket. Given her state of mind, any airline would prefer giving someone their money back to having a potentially dangerous-when-crazy passenger aboard. Her tactic worked. American Airlines refunded my three hundred and fifty-two dollars, no questions asked.

Chapter 42
Derek

Siobhan started cheating on her boyfriends when she was sixteen, hooking up with her friend Derek while she was still dating Chris.

Derek was impertinent and a bad influence. On a mission to cause unhappiness, he spat negative epithets, and wore a permanent sinister scowl. His uniform of dingy jeans and a black trench coat told the world he didn't care, so get out of his way or watch out! I hated this guy.

He hated me too. He thought I was supercilious simply because I smiled and went to college. But he was a huge loser, so I didn't care.

Siobhan kept anyone around who would stay, no matter how they treated her. After all, she manically sped from one extreme emotion to the other for no apparent reason, so if she found someone willing to return for more drama time and time again she welcomed them back with open arms. This was the case with Derek.

They began officially dating after Chris broke up with her for cheating. A twenty-year chaotic cycle continues to this day.

Not surprisingly Derek became physically abusive. But I'm not sure I blame him entirely. Sibby was too, after all. In fact, she sickly *wanted* him to hit her. Her mania craved turmoil. Then she had a crisis. Her mental illness *loved* a crisis.

"Derek beat the shit out of me last night," she cried to me on the phone in 2008. She was twenty three years old. "But I

Voicemails from My Sister

fought back, Kate. You would've been proud of me. I fought back," she collapsed into uncontrollable sobs.

The police report told the real story.

Sibby had struck Derek first. He hit back in self-defense. Siobhan had instigated the whole thing. Our mother used to do that to our father.

"You've got to kick him out of your life completely," I instructed my sister, trying to be supportive.

"I know. I will. I'm never going to see him again," she assured.

Two weeks later the same thing happened again.

The couple would get arrested, one would file a restraining order against the other, then they'd be back together by the end of the week.

Bipolar schizoaffective disorder loves excitement.

It makes perfect sense. Siobhan was abused, so she became abusive, and courts fellow abusers. Then, in order to feel triumphant, she cheats on them. This soothes her subconscious, so she no longer feels like a victim, but instead like the winner of the relationship. She comes out on top because she is hurting her partner in a way they weren't expecting. They were expecting physical abuse, but not cheating. If they cried, that enlarged Sibby's head even more, assuring her that she had the power to make someone feel so deeply that they were overwhelmed to the point of tears.

Some people with bipolar schizoaffective disorder have very low self-esteem, so they love being made to feel tall with importance. They will manipulate situations to achieve this feeling.

Likewise they also love the roller coaster ride of being on top of the world one minute, then in a heap of tears the next. Why else would Sibby return to the same abusive, chaotic relationship time and time again?

Again, it makes perfect sense. Our parents were happy one minute and beating us the next, so she is conditioned to live in that environment. Of course she gravitates towards people who provide the same unpredictability.

And so the cycle continues.

Chapter 43
My Package

"I'm gonna send your Christmas package," Sibby would claim. "I just have to get a ride to the post office."

It was an ongoing declaration. For years Siobhan asserted that she had a Christmas, birthday, Valentine's Day box for me, that she would send as soon as someone else got their shit together and gave her a ride. In 2010, six years after she allegedly began putting this gift together, I finally got it.

"What a thoughtful assortment of gifts," I wrote in a thank you card. "I so appreciate that you took the time to put it together."

A random conglomeration of odds and ends made up the contents of the, for some reason, damp cardboard box. A pile of beaded bracelets that she'd strung together just for me topped the gift basket. "They're real emeralds," she'd professed, regarding the green plastic bulbs. I was touched. I put them on and dug into the carton. Pushing aside a few random packing peanuts, I found one of my old Sweet Valley High books, Volume 28, *Leaving Home*. Underneath lay a broken picture frame with an image of me and Sibby as babies, an empty Zippo with a worn out flint wheel, and a single gold-plated dangle earring. A single serving of Bazooka gum was melting onto a loose, unlabeled CD. And finally, an empty envelope with my name written on it sat atop a cigarette butt.

"Was there supposed to be a card in that envelope?" I asked my sister, trying not to sound judgmental.

Voicemails from My Sister

"I was gonna write you a letter but ran out of time," she explained.

Chapter 44
Striphilis

"How've you been?" my thirty-five-year-old sister asked me in one of our intermittent phone calls.

"I've been sick, actually," I answered.

"I'll bet it's not as bad as what I have," she replied.

Here we go. Should I even bother? "What do you have, Sibby?"

"Syphilis."

I sighed. The only surprising part of this diagnosis was how long it took her to get it.

"Sibby, why aren't you having protected sex?" I asked her.

"No, I got it from the stripper pole," she explained, as if that were somehow better.

My sister periodically gyrated during the breakfast shift at an all-nude dive joint on the Berlin turnpike. Unable to hold a steady job, she'd been picking up sub-par stage time at this sleazy hole since she was eighteen. Our father actually used to drop her off there once in awhile back then, supporting his perverse theory that any job was better than no job. Now she "danced" when someone would give her a ride there. Sometimes she'd pay a "friend" twenty dollars just to bring her to work, then leave six hours later with a whopping ten. How did she get home, you ask? She'd hit up customers for rides,

Voicemails from My Sister

offering to pay them, even though she was already in the red.

I say she "danced," but you really couldn't call it that. My poor sister had no rhythm, flexibility, or strength whatsoever, so all she really did was tweak naked until she tripped on her shoes and fell off the stage. The cost of occupational injuries she sustained from this career choice had far outweighed her actual income.

Years earlier a guy she was dating carried her into the diner where I worked because her high heels had given her water on the knee, and she was unable to walk. Her six-foot tall beau cradled one hundred and thirty pound Sibby like a baby in his arms as he ascended the steps into my restaurant. He set her down on her good foot and she hopped to a booth, garnering the attention of diners and causing my face to turn red. Sibby's brain didn't know when to get embarrassed, and she proceeded as if everyone *wasn't* staring at her. When they left I neurotically stopped him from picking her up again, and helped her limp out to the car with him. She went into work that night on crutches, but, to her dismay, the owner would not permit her to perform with the props.

"Gross, Sibby, you're supposed to clean that pole between dancers," I informed my disgusting sibling.

"I know, they're supposed to clean it." She immediately blamed someone else. "But they didn't and now I have Syphilis and I might die." She began getting worked up.

"You're not gonna die, Sibby. You must've gone to the doctor to get diagnosed. Didn't they give you any medicine?" I was becoming impatient.

Voicemails from My Sister

"Yes, they gave me medicine for it, but I left it at the club because my boss made me put it in a drawer and you know how I am — out of sight, out of mind — so it's been three days now and I haven't had my medicine and my friend who is friends with my boss's brother got out of work at midnight and was supposed to go get it for me but now I can't get ahold of him, so I might die." She laughed monotonously. Like a deranged robot. "You know me, always trying to keep a sense of humor. But he didn't bring the medicine at midnight, is the point."

"Oh my God, Sibby," I sighed.

She burst into tears. "I know and this might be the last phone call because I can't leave the house because the angel of death might have a hit out on me."

"Jesus Christ, Sibby."

"I know, and so that's why I'm calling."

"Sibby, I can guarantee there's no hit out on you."

"You can? Thank you!" She continued to bawl.

"Go to the hospital," I continued.

"I can't because I'd have to go to Meriden and I don't have enough gas."

"Why do you have to go to Meriden?"

"Because I'm not going to Middlesex after they stole Gumma's ring, plus I tried to go there and the intake woman couldn't ask me a question the right way and there was a

Voicemails from My Sister

security officer behind me and they kicked me out when I got pissed at her and I said, 'well fine, fuck you guys.'"

"OK, well, I guess you're gonna die then."

"OK, well thank you for taking the call."

"I'll pray for you."

Chapter 45
Ghost Baby

I hadn't spoken to my dad in eight years when I got his text in 2018. "Can you call me when you get a sec? We need to discuss the properties."

My father and his cousin co-owned four houses in Middletown: Gumma's house, 145, and two other houses on Bend Lane. My father had lived in Gumma's house for years. He and Mary Jo rented out the other three.

Nervous, I called him.

He was sweet as pie: "How've you been? How's the career? The love life?" I reverted back to perpetrator-pleasing and smiled as I pleasantly answered his queries. "Anyway, the reason I'm calling… over the years Mary Jo and I have depleted the estate account and reached into our own pockets to foot the bill for the many various repairs the houses have needed: a new roof, new septic system, etcetera. As of right now the estate account is empty and we have spent seventy thousand dollars of our own money. At this point it makes the most sense to sell 145, recoup our losses, and put the balance in the estate account, as more repairs are inevitable," he explained diplomatically. "The problem is, the way Gumma wrote her will, if I sell the house, the money automatically goes to you and Siobhan. So, what I'd like you to do is gift the house to me and, once I sell it, I'll give each of you five thousand dollars for your troubles," he said with a condescending scoff. "Now, you can refuse, but then Mary Jo and I can sue you," he began to threaten, "to get back the money we've already sunk into the houses. I'd rather not do that."

Voicemails from My Sister

I didn't want to fight, and what he said sounded reasonable. I agreed.

"Now, can you convince Sibby to sell?"

He hadn't spoken to her in years. Of course he wasn't willing to swallow his pride to do so now. He'd rather send me to do his dirty work.

"No. It's not *my* job."

"Punkie, she won't talk to me. I figure, you have a good relationship with her. Maybe she'll listen to you."

The possibility of five grand tempted me. I called her.

"Sibby, look, Dad wants to sell 145 Bend Lane," I explained the situation.

"No, Punkie, I can't sell that house."

I sighed. *Christ. Here we go.* "Why not, Sibby?"

"... Never mind."

"No, Sibby." I raised my voice. "This is important. Why not?"

"Because the ghost of my dead son is in that house, alright!?" she yelled back at me. "When I was pregnant and Derek threw me down the stairs, I lost the baby," she continued on with her delusion. "His spirit haunts that house. I'll never sell that house! Fuck Dad!"

Siobhan had never been pregnant at that point.

Voicemails from My Sister

"Look Sibby, let's just call the estate manager and hear what she has to say before we make any decisions, OK?" I steered her back to the real world.

Together, we called Burdom & Burdom, the company that had been handling the estate account for years, and spoke to Samantha, the account manager. She confirmed what my father had said: the estate account was empty, and it made the most sense to sell one of the properties to prepare for future repairs of the other three houses.

"What about selling a different house?" I asked her, so that Sibby could hear the answer.

"145 has the smallest amount of land attached to it, so it makes the most sense to sell that one."

"Let me ask you a question," Sibby began astutely. "Have there been any ghost sightings in that house?"

Samantha paused, " … Not to my knowledge, no," she replied as non-judgmentally as possible.

"OK, thank you, we'll discuss it and get back to you," I quickly interjected.

We hung up with Samantha.

"So, it's all legit, Sibs. I think we should do it. I mean, we're gonna inherit these houses anyway, and we're gonna have to put money into the repairs either way. It makes the most sense to just liquidate this one now so Dad and Mary Jo can repair them sooner rather than later."

"… Yeah," she agreed. "OK, you're right, it makes sense."

Voicemails from My Sister

"OK, so I'll tell Dad we agree."

"OK."

Two days later she called me in a rage. "You can tell your father I said he can go fuck himself! I'm not selling that house! Let him sue me! He's not my real father anyway!"

All that had changed in the past forty-eight hours was that Sibby had allowed herself to fall down the rabbit hole of negative thinking. Mania had overtaken her mind and stirred up controversy. Her diseased thinking reminded her that she hated her father, and the Abilify she took daily peppered her memories with delusions.

"Sibby, calm down," I tried to talk her off the ledge, but she was way beyond the point of reason.

"NO! FUCK YOU AND EDDIE TOO! YOU'RE BOTH TRYING TO MAKE ME THINK I'M CRAZY! YOU'RE IN THIS TOGETHER! I'LL NEVER GIVE YOU WHAT YOU WANT!" she screamed, wielding the power she held.

"STOP YELLING AT ME!" She remained the one person who could make me livid.

I imagined her smile at my outburst. She loved chaos.

"You and Eddie have always been against me." She excitedly allowed her madness to take her on a ride. "When I was a baby you cursed me. You thought I didn't know about it, but I did. But I reversed the spell. You didn't know I could do that, but I did."

I had to get off this ride.

Voicemails from My Sister

"Whatever Sibby." I hung up.

Chapter 46
Blocking the Crazy

On May 9, 2019 I received the following message from my sister on Facebook:

Btw the same guy that raped you raped me recently. I tried to reach out to you. I'm not kidding Wish I was. You were right, it's his m.o. Hope you find him. New London is where he was staying. You were his victim too. If you care at all about me have him put away. For what its worth I still love you and I'm sorry we argue so much. I apologize. And you were right, he is not skinny and does not look the same. He targeted me. He told me to my face. I swear to God. I'm not bullshitting you at all. I'm scared and alone. I tried to fight back. He held me down so I couldn't move or get up. I swear this is not in any way a joke.

I blocked her on Facebook, then called her.

"Sibby, I've never been raped." I was angry. Her disease had overtaken her and I was mad that I was so heavily involved in this phantasm.

"I understand why you'd deny it," she began.

"No," I retorted. "I am not denying it, Sibby. You are having a delusion."

"I'm not delusional! I don't have schizoaffective disorder. I'm bipolar," she continued.

Voicemails from My Sister

"If that were true you wouldn't be having delusions that I told you I was raped," I spat back. "I never told you that because it isn't true."

"Yes, you did." She fought back. "You're denying it now because you want me to think I'm crazy."

"I don't want you to think you're crazy, you ARE crazy!" I argued.

She hung up.

I didn't speak to her again for five months.

Chapter 47
Rape Baby

On October 28, 2019, Sibby left me the following voicemail: "Hi Kate, this is your sister Siobhan Russell. Um, I'm calling you from the hospital in New Britain HOCC, which is — " she stopped a passerby, " — what does HOCC stand for? ... Hospital of Central Connecticut. Hospital of Central Connecticut, HOCC. I'm in EW4, I'm in the mental ward, but that's not the reason I'm calling. I'm pregnant sixteen weeks with a baby from what I told you was an incident of rape and I need your help urgently. So Kate, seriously, I need you to call me as soon as you get this message. This is serious and this is not a joke. No puns. No bullshit. Kate, this is serious. I really am pregnant and I need your help. And I'm so sorry for what I said before. I completely apologize for the last conversation we had months ago, but I haven't spoken to you since and a lot of weird things have been going on. But I need you, Kate. You're my sister. You're my only living relative that I can trust, so please," she started sobbing uncontrollably, "don't let me down. Please! Kate, I love you and I'm sorry about the way we spoke to each other. I'm sorry for my part and I love you with all my heart. Please help."

No. I was not getting on this ride again. I did not call her back.

The following day she called again. When I didn't answer she left the following message: "Kate, it's Sibby. I'm calling because I'm in a hospital. I am possibly pregnant and it's definitely four months, is what they think. And, um, I hope you're OK given the fires on the news and I — I pray for you every day now that I'm in the hospital, and I hope you're surviving and OK. I love you very much and I need your support and I need your help so call the hospital — New Britain hospital it's called — um, what is it called here?" she asked again, "Hospital of Central Connecticut. And it's really me, it's Sibby, and I — I love you and I need your support right now. Thank you. Bye bye."

My ex, Austin, who spoke to Sibby periodically, called me. "Sibby is sixteen weeks pregnant with the rapist's baby," he informed me.

"I heard," I answered blankly. I was skeptical because fifty percent of the things that came out of Sibby's mouth were misbeliefs. "But we don't know if she was really raped, or if it's all just fantasy. The last time I talked to Sibby she had a whole delusional memory of me telling her that *I* was raped. She was hallucinating."

"I know," he sympathized. "Well, you could at least call her nurse and find out if she is, in fact, pregnant."

I did.

"Yes, Siobhan is sixteen weeks along," she confirmed. "She'll be held here indefinitely, then transferred to Connecticut Valley Hospital until she gives birth." As Siobhan was a ward of the state, they had a legal responsibility to her fetus. They had to make sure Sibby was taken care of until she gave birth. If something went wrong while she was carrying, potential lawsuits were aplenty, ranging from birth defects as the result of improper or inconsistent medication during her pregnancy, to miscarriages. The state might be underfunded when it came to good health care for their patients, but when it came to lawyers, they had the best money could buy. No way would my sister be let out of sight until she delivered a healthy child.

"Looks like I'm going to be an aunty," I joked to Austin.

"I think you should talk to her and see if she's considered the… alternatives," he replied.

Goddammit. He was right. This was about the baby, not about me and my sister's dysfunctional relationship. There was no way she could care for a baby, so it'd just end up in foster care. Her psychiatric problems were surely genetic, and the father was possibly a rapist, which meant he had less-than-ideal genes as well… I called her.

"Hello," she sounded catatonic.

"Hi Sibby, it's Kate."

She immediately started to cry. "I'm so sorry for all the times we fought and for all the mean stuff I said to you," she began repeating her messages.

"I know, I know. It's fine, just forget it." I wanted to avoid drama.

We spoke for a few minutes. She told me the hospital was awful. She couldn't smoke and they wouldn't even give her a nicotine patch. She sounded very tired.

"They took me off Abilify and put me on Haldol," she explained. "I hate it. It makes me a zombie. I drool on myself."

I felt so sad for her my chest ached.

"Look, Sibs, have you considered … getting an abortion?"

Voicemails from My Sister

"I *would've* considered it," she began, "but it's too late. I'm already in the second trimester."

I hadn't thought of that. "OK, well, what about putting it up for adoption?" I continued.

"Yes, I know a couple who might want to adopt the child. Peg and Frank. They're married. I went to their wedding. She can't have kids, but they want one so they said they might want to adopt the baby if they can afford a lawyer. And that would be good because then I could remain in the baby's life," she reasoned.

That *would* be good, actually. It would break my sister's heart to have to give up her baby and never see it again. And, although she was crazy, she wasn't evil. She would love that baby. If she didn't have to raise it, but could visit and give it love… that *could* be ideal.

A month later I called these prospective parents.

"Hello," Peg squawked into the phone, before dropping it. "Oh, son of a bitch," I heard her exclaim as she shuffled around what sounded like a pile of papers, looking for the phone. She finally found it. "HELLO!" she yelled into the receiver, as if *I* were responsible for her clumsiness.

"Hi, Peg? It's Kate, Siobhan's sister," I began.

"What? Oh, hi," She was still discombobulated.

"I just thought I'd give you a call to talk about the adoption," I continued.

"Who is it?" I heard a male voice, presumably Frank, mutter in the background.

"It's Siobhan's sister," Peg snapped.

"I just wondered what was going on with the lawyer, because Sibby said there was a problem…" They had spent all five hundred dollars of their savings, according to my sister, on hiring a lawyer to represent them in court without ever contacting the Department of Child and Family Services to begin the vetting process. When their court date arrived they showed up with a lawyer, but no DCF approval. In other words, they had no idea what they were doing. The hearing was rescheduled, as this couple was unprepared, but now they had no money to go through the process again.

"Yeah, we didn't know we had to call DCF," Peg shouted defensively. "No one told us anything. Then this lawyer, he just takes our money and says, 'sorry, you pay me for my time,' so now we're out our entire life savings!"

I sighed. On one hand, it sucked that this potential family fell through, but on the other, they didn't seem like ideal candidates.

Siobhan was transferred from New Britain Hospital back to Connecticut Valley Hospital, the psychiatric facility located across the street from my father's house.

"I can see Dad's backyard when we're allowed outside on our free hour," she told me.

Wow, I thought. *Sometimes truth really is stranger than fiction.* I couldn't make this shit up.

Voicemails from My Sister

"When was the last time you spoke to him?" I asked out of curiosity.

"I climbed through his window a few months ago," she answered, like it was nothing. "I had a feeling that he was not OK, so I walked to his house at four a.m. and knocked on the back door. He was asleep in the chair, so I climbed through the window in the kitchen," she continued.

"So, you broke in?" I charged.

"No, I climbed through the window," she clarified.

My mistake. "Go on."

"He was breathing, so I went into the living room and fell asleep on the couch. He woke me up at six a.m. and said, 'what are you doing here?' so I told him I was worried about him and he said I could stay there until nine because I had my River Valley Services appointment at nine."

I wondered if my father knew his youngest daughter was currently institutionalized in a facility within spitting distance of his house. It wouldn't matter either way. He'd never visit her.

I talked to Sibby almost every day over the next few months, and we'd FaceTime when her social worker would let her use her cell phone instead of the patient phone in the common room. I couldn't remember *ever* having such a consistently good rapport with my sister.

"Sibs, I just wanted to point out that our relationship has dramatically improved over the past few months. We have thirty-minute conversations regularly now. We couldn't talk for thirty *seconds* before you were in the hospital." I cited the source. "I know you don't like Haldol, but honey, it helps with your figments. You don't think untrue things, you're not manic, and you don't seem too drowsy anymore, either. I think you just needed to get used to the Haldol, and now it's really working for you."

"I know," she agreed. "But I'm going to go back on the Abilify when I leave here. I think it's the anti-anxiety pill that helps me, not the Haldol."

"OK," I said, but I was skeptical.

Janice, Sibby's DCF case worker, called me in March. "There is a new family interested in adopting the baby." Kenny and Sean had two adopted children through the Connecticut foster system already, and were looking to complete their family with one more. Both professors, they had summers off, which they filled with family vacations. Their two young children, Daniel and Autumn, had already been to both Disney World *and* Disney Land. The family was spending their Coronavirus quarantine all together at their summer beach house with their two dogs and two cats. A smattering of chickens completed their clan back home at their fall, winter and spring house.

Kenny and Sean wanted an open adoption. "You are the only mother Damien will ever know," they assured Sibby, in an introduction letter. "You will always be a part of his life. He will know where he came from, and you will be part of the family."

"Sibby, this family is a gift from God," I told my sister.

"I know," she agreed.

Damien Elijah was born on April Fool's Day, 2020.

Voicemails from My Sister

"Congratulations, mama!" I called her a few hours after the C-section.

"Thank you! Punkie, he's so cute!" she sounded drunk. "When they took him out he cried and I smiled," she continued. "Hold on — I'm gonna be sick," she said to the nurse presumably standing at her bedside. I heard her vomit into a bucket.

"Sorry, Punkie. They gave me Fentanyl and it makes me sick to my stomach."

"They gave you *Fentanyl?*" I exclaimed.

"Yeah, I'm completely numb. I didn't feel anything except the epidural needle. Then I was pretty much out the entire delivery. Except when I heard him cry. Then I smiled and woke up."

I was so proud of her, and I hadn't expected to feel that way. My sister, who uses Nair instead of shaving her legs because she's terrified of nicking herself with a razor, had successfully delivered a healthy baby boy. I was an aunt… and I was excited. I hadn't had a good relationship with Siobhan in years. But now that we had reestablished a real connection, I felt a connection to her son as well. I let myself feel that excitement. I allowed fantasy to take over. I couldn't wait to spoil him! To kiss his tiny face! To hold him and give him squishes and love! I wanted to start a college fund for him, and buy him all of the books I loved when I was a kid. I wanted to visit him while he was still tiny and sing him lullabies like Nana and Gumma used to sing me. I wanted to buy him baby clothes with stupid sayings like, "My Aunt Rocks" on them. My heart was full.

Voicemails from My Sister

"Maybe I'll come home for Thanksgiving so I can meet him," I proposed.

"That would be wonderful, Punkie!"

For a few minutes it was fun to pretend my sister and I finally had an ideal family. Maybe it wasn't too late...

Siobhan was released from CVH mid-May. She'd been temporarily reassigned back to the mental facility after giving birth because of the Coronavirus pandemic, but was now free to go back to her apartment.

And, just as she'd threatened, she immediately stopped taking Haldol and went back on Abilify.

She'd been home two weeks when she called me in a panic. "Kate, I have genital warts," she announced. Her nervous disorder was back. Her anxiety was running her mouth.

"Christ, Sibby, when did you find this out?"

"Two days ago. I went back to the doctor — I had to get a ride from Paul, I paid him twenty dollars — anyway, he took me back to Middlesex and they did a test and they said," she decreased to a whisper, "that I have genital warts."

She was paranoid someone was listening. I sighed. She was going crazy again. I knew this would happen.

Her new conservator, Paul, was a drifter she barely knew. Jobless and alcoholic, she'd assigned him the task of managing her finances because, "the state was stealing from her," and Paul was going to assist her in becoming financially independent.

Voicemails from My Sister

"How do you know he's not going to steal from you, Sibs? I mean, being a conservator is a big job. He might decide he deserves a salary for it and take your money without you knowing. Then what could you do?"

"He won't, Kate. He's trustworthy."

Of course. They all were.

I detached.

At the end of June Sibby called, frantic. "I have bad news. I saw pictures of the baby and he looks like Jake." Jake, a fellow ne'er-do-well, was one of her friends with benefits. "We had sex before I was raped and he came in me."

"And you didn't think the baby could be his until *now*?" I scolded.

"No, I did! I told him I thought I was pregnant and he ghosted me. I haven't talked to him since then. But I told Janice that I thought it could be Jake's and she's legally got to order a paternity test and if Jake refuses to take it they can court mandate it and if he's the father then his mom will want to take the baby. I know her, Kate, she's crazy and she hates me. But she'll want to raise the baby even if Jake doesn't and because she's a blood relative DCF will choose her over Kenny and Sean."

"*Why* did you tell Janice!?" I yelled. "Why would you potentially screw up your child's future?"

Because she was on drugs that made her unpredictable and destructive. Just like our mother.

"She had a right to know, Kate!" she screamed defensively. That made no sense. She was all defensiveness. No logic. She was just defending the poor choice she'd made because her Abilify-driven brain made it, not because it was the right thing to do.

I called Kenny and Sean. "We've been through this before," they talked me down. "They might put an ad out in the paper asking Jake to take a paternity test, but if he doesn't show up they won't pursue it. Don't worry. They'll do what's best for Damien." They had two children through DCF already so their words put me at ease.

Chapter 48
Do You Want the Good News or the Bad News?

"Punkie," she began, frantically, "I have good news and bad news. What do you want first?"

I did not want to encourage her. "Sibby, just tell me."

"OK, the bad news is: when the guy broke into my apartment and raped me, he stabbed me in the heart with a needle and it broke off in my heart, and they can't remove it because I went to Middlesex Hospital and they said, 'I'm sorry but there's nothing we can do,' and I said, 'OK I'll just deal with it,' so I might die at any given time because of this."

How was I supposed to react? "… OK"

"So, if I move in any way at any given time the needle could pierce my heart and I could die. Rather than believe me you'd rather doubt me, which really hurts."

It was as if she were reading my mind.

"The guy that raped me stabbed me in the heart with a fucking needle and it broke off in my fucking heart and I could die at any moment!" she repeated.

I was triggered. How *should* I react? "What kind of needle?"

That just made her mad. "I don't know what kind of needle because I never saw it! I went to Middlesex four weeks ago and got a chest x-ray. I might never get to see my kid again if I die!"

Voicemails from My Sister

"How much Abilify are you taking?"

"I take twenty milligrams a day," she answered calmly, trying to prove she was in her right mind. But then she continued, "I can't get the needle removed because it's in the center of my heart, acting as a valve. And I also just pulled a bot fly off my body last night which is native to Central America and the maintenance guy is Columbian so he could've brought it in with him. He was in my apartment doing a nutmeg inspection and it's been parasite-ing off my back."

"When was the last time you smoked pot?" I asked. I was taking notes.

"Two days ago. If I go back to Middlesex they'll put me in North Seven because I'm anxiety through the roof." Suddenly, she switched gears, "Anyway, the good news is I got your birthday present in the mail. Do you want to know what it is?"

I couldn't wait.

"It's a Lady Gaga CD, Fame Monster. I know you know I'm like Lady Gaga in many ways."

I already had that album downloaded on my computer and iPhone. "... I don't have a CD player, Sibby."

"Oh shit. Oh, no!" she whined.

"Can you return it?" I knew she couldn't. She was incapable of doing any menial task, but, as she explained it, she didn't have a ride to the post office.

"No, I bought it off eBay. No returns. So if I can't use it oh well, I'll just suffer." She returned to the tumult. It was more fun. "Anyway, I was scared because the rapist was a hit on

Voicemails from My Sister

my life. They're targeting me to kill me. But I talked my way out of it. He agreed to leave me alone and never come back. I spoke psycho to him. Psycho-babble. I acted my way out of a paper bag, so to speak. He was sent here to kill me because I had an affair with a married man."

Should I ask?

"What married man, Sibby?"

"That's classified."

My energy had dropped substantially since the start of this phone call, as I instinctually sought balance. I had to get off. I was only encouraging her. "OK, Sibby. I gotta go."

"Of course you do. You always have to go." She hated when people wouldn't humor her psychosis.

I hung up.

I called Gilead, Sibby's new state-funded mental health program. I wanted to speak to her psychiatrist.

"She has to sign a release in order for Anne to speak to you," the assistant told me.

"I have one," I explained. I'd spoken to her doctors regularly while she was in CVH.

"Actually, she has to sign a new one since she's with Gilead now. The release for CVH and her old program, River Valley services, doesn't transfer," she explained.

"But she *won't* sign a new release *now* because she's paranoid because she's taking the wrong medication, which is what I need to talk to her psychiatrist *about*." I knew this was a dead end.

I was right.

"No way." Sibby exerted the power she thought she held. "I won't let you talk to my doctors because you just want to put me back on the Haldol because you think I'm crazy."

Well, she was right, except that my intentions were good, not evil. I didn't want to control her or sedate her. I just wanted my sister back.

A few weeks passed, then I FaceTimed with Kenny and Sean. "Have you talked to Siobhan?" I asked Sean.

"No, she keeps missing our scheduled FaceTime calls. She was actually supposed to come for a visit but then said she couldn't because her friend threw a recluse spider on her as a joke and it bit her and now venom is coursing through her veins."

Yeah, that sounded about right.

"Jesus Christ."

I wondered if, deep down, beneath her crazy, she was afraid to see Damien again because it'd break her heart. I wondered if her brain was protecting her from the heartbreak of having to give her baby, who she hadn't seen since birth, back to the family that gets to raise him after a short, monitored visit. I wondered if she knew it'd be too painful to see him again, since she can't keep him, so her diseased mind was inventing reasons why she couldn't see him again. I wouldn't doubt it. The brain constructs defenses to protect us from pain. This would be a painful situation.

Chapter 49
I'm Sorry

"Punkie, I'm sorry Dad raped you. He raped me, too. Mom took me out of state to have the baby."

"None of that happened, Sibby," I replied flatly.

"It didn't?"

"Nope."

She'd been back on Abilify for two months, and was crazier than ever.

"Listen, I can't talk to you when you're delusional," I began.

"I'M NOT DELUSIONAL! I DON'T HAVE SCHIZOAFFECTIVE DISORDER! I'M BIPOLAR, JUST LIKE MOM!"

Oh, she was just like our mom, alright. I hung up.

Chapter 50
It's Only Getting Worse

I began answering her calls only occasionally, after asking myself if I was mentally prepared to handle whatever degree of crazy might be on the other end of the line.

"I'm coming clean about this now. I was the victim of a crime when I was sixteen and Mom covered it up. I was hit in the back of the head with a shovel."

Nothing phased me at this point.

"By who, Sibby?"

"I still don't know. Mom was the witness."

"Sibby, you know that's not true." I don't know why I even bothered to argue. I just couldn't pretend her fantasies were real. Who would that benefit?

"No, it is true. I had an x-ray and the doctor even said, 'if your sister could see this X-ray she'd believe you and know you need medical, not mental health disability. You need a nurse there to take care of you 24/7…' There's marks all over my body that just appeared and I don't know what they are. They keep appearing. I don't know if it's bed bugs. So I have to go back to the doctor to find out."

Good God. I had to change the subject. Austin had told me she'd gotten a job.

"Are you still working at McDonald's?"

Voicemails from My Sister

"Well, technically I missed my first day because I went to Middlesex and the manager fired me because he told me not to go to Middlesex and I did and he said, 'oh hell no, she's fucking fired.'"

"Sibby, the manager of McDonald's didn't fire you because you went to Middlesex. He fired you because you never showed up to your first day of work."

"..."

OK, new topic.

"What's going on with Damien and the adoption and DCF?"

"Damien is not Jake's baby, it's the rapist's. I know because the cops came to my door and told me somebody came forth and admitted to being the rapist, so they arrested him and now he's in jail."

"What do you mean someone admitted to being the rapist?"

"He came to see me at the hospital when I was pregnant because he wanted to be tested for paternity."

"... Oh, for Christ's sake."

I knew this was another delusion. Redirect the discussion again. I had seen pictures of a scrapbook someone had made for her of pictures of her son.

"Who gave you those scrapbooks of pictures of Damien?"

"Jennifer. But she took them."

Voicemails from My Sister

"Jennifer gave you scrapbooks of pictures of your son and then took them back?"

"Yeah... or they could be on the coffee table."

Chapter 51
I Get It

"I want to start you on a low dose of Abilify," my psychiatrist said. "It can help major depressive disorder."

"I don't know…" I hesitated. "That's what my sister's on and she's crazy."

"Well, you don't have schizoaffective disorder, and in cases where antidepressants fail, the addition of a low dose of Abilify can help stimulate the antidepressant and relieve the patient's depression."

I began taking two milligrams of Abilify a day, in addition to the 20 milligrams of Lexapro that I was already taking… and I suddenly understood why my sister loves it.

I felt elated! Like I was on speed again. My compulsive behaviors increased and I couldn't sleep, but I wasn't tired and was getting so much done!

Maybe Sibby was a drug addict like me. This was certainly a feeling I wanted to hang onto.

What's more important to me? How I feel or how others perceive me? I asked myself. *How I feel, of course.*

Well then, no wonder Sibby didn't care if I thought the Abilify made her neurotic and paranoid. She felt ecstatic. Now I understood.

I called my sister to commiserate.

Voicemails from My Sister

"The God-damned landlord wants to charge me to replace my door because I had to break it down!" She was enraged.

"Why did you have to break it down?"

"Because I lost my key."

I paused.

"So why didn't you just call her to let you in?" I attempted to remain patient.

"I did, Kate! But it was the middle of the night and she said she couldn't get here for a few hours!"

I took another beat as I pondered how to respond. But Sibby continued.

"And there was no way I was gonna wait in my hallway for two fucking hours for this dumb bitch!"

I sighed. Silently so she couldn't hear.

"But now she wants me to pay for that shit? No way! Fuck her! I'm not paying for it! She shoulda gotten here sooner!"

"So now you have no door?" I asked.

"No, but my friend Liam sleeps outside in the hallway at night to make sure no one tries to get in."

Never mind. I excused myself. "OK, well, I hope you figure it out. I gotta go, Sibby. I love you."

Voicemails from My Sister

"OK, well, I guess you don't want to hear about how my neck was broken last night after a domestic altercation. But that's OK. My friend was able to fix most of the damage."

I couldn't bond with Sibby over our new commonality. She was too far gone.

Chapter 52
What it's Like Now

"I live on only sixty dollars a week," Sibby bewailed. Of course that's after all of her bills and groceries are taken care of. Through social security disability she is left with sixty dollars spending money per week.

"That's more than I get," I said. I'd been out of work for eleven months due to Covid. I was making four hundred and fifty dollars a week, but still had to pay all of my own bills. If I hadn't had savings I would've been deep in debt by now.

But Sibby wasn't listening. She was making a point. "Yeah, so I've had to struggle to even put gas in my car," she continued. She now had a working vehicle. God help the other drivers on the snowy roads of Middletown.

I remained silent. A beat. Then, "Punkie, I have to ask you something."

There it was. I knew she was going to ask me to send her food.

"What?" I replied, tentatively.

Her voice softened. "Could you possibly send me Newfield Pizza tonight?"

I sighed. What should I do? *Just say yes,* the God voice in my head replied, *before you have a chance to make excuses or to yell at her about your own financial struggles.*

"OK, what do you want?" I obeyed the voice in my head.

Voicemails from My Sister

"Thank you," she answered.

"You're welcome. What do you want?" I was triggered, as usual, by her call.

"A mandarin chicken salad and a cheese pizza," she replied.

I called Newfield Pizza. "I want to order delivery, but I want to pay with a credit card over the phone because I'm not there. I'm sending food to my sister," I explained to the woman who answered the phone.

"Um, OK, hold on," she said. I went through this every time.

A few minutes later she picked up again. "OK, I just had to check with my manager. That's fine. What would you like?"

Was I enabling my sister? She likely had food, or money with which to buy herself takeout. *Everyone deserves a treat now and then,* the God voice argued. *You don't send her food that much anymore, so it's a nice gesture.*

"Give a man a fish, he eats for a day. Teach a man to fish, he eats for a lifetime," our father used to say… But he hadn't taught Sibby how to fish. And I certainly couldn't either.

How long before Sibby's diseased brain manipulates this good deed into something bad? I wondered. *Well, I'll only do it once in awhile,* I reasoned.

A month later, as I predicted, my kindness turned around to bite me in the ass.

"You poisoned me!"

Voicemails from My Sister

I sighed. "What are you talking about, Sibby?"

"You put blood and piss and shit and cum in my food!"

Wow.

"Gross, Sibby. And how did I do that? I'm 3,000 miles away."

"You had a will and found a way," she hissed.

"Oh for Christ's sake. *Why* would I do that?"

"To try to kill me!"

Her brain had mangled another good deed. Her bipolar schizoaffective disorder just won't allow anything to remain pure.

She won't remember this accusation tomorrow. We'll go on as if it never happened.

I pray for my sister, but realize that God's will, not mine, will be done. I maintain a healthy distance, only answering her calls when I'm emotionally prepared to handle whatever state of crazy she may be in.

My sister is a good person. She's just sick, and there is nothing I can do to change that.

I take care of myself by maintaining boundaries.

Maybe she is living her best life. Who am I to judge? I only know what's best for me. But she and I are different, so what's best for me isn't necessarily what's best for her. Only God knows what's best for her. I leave it to Him.

Made in the USA
Columbia, SC
07 July 2022